Towards Social Movement Unionism?

.

Towards Social Movement Unionism?

How labour organisations can succeed in a globalised era

DR JOHN ALAN DODD
PhD, FRSA, FinstLM

ISBN 978-1-9164638-0-6

Cover design copyright © 2018 AAD GeOMiLa
Cover image by Ikatod – Freepik.com

Printed in the UK

10 9 8 7 6 5 4 3 2 1

For Alessandro 'Alex' Alan Dodd and his Mam

Thanks to all of you who have helped along the way (especially Alan and Joyce Dodd). Too many names and too many roles to list.

Thank you x

Table of Contents

ABBREVIATIONS

AEEU	Amalgamated Engineering and Electrical Union
AFL-CIO	American Federation of Labor-Congress of Industrial Organizations
CBI	Council for Business and Industry
CCC	Clean Clothes Campaign
ECPE	European Centre for Public Enterprises
DGB	Deutscher Gewerkschaftsbund
DTI	Department of Trade and Industry
ECJ	European Court of Justice
EEN	European Employers' Network
EFILWC	European Foundation for the Improvement of Living and Working Conditions
EIF	European Industry Federation
EIO	European Industrial Relations Observatory
EPZ	Export Processing Zones
ETUC	European Trade Union Confederation
EU	European Union
EQC	European Works Council
FDI	Foreign Direct Investment
GCS	Global Civil Society
GMB	General Manufacturing and Boilermakers Union
G7	Group of Seven
G77	Group of Seventy Seven Developing Countries
GPE	Global Political Economy
ICFTU	International Confederation of Free Trade Unions.
ITGWF	International Textile, Garment and Leather Workers Federation
ILO	International Labour Organisation
IPE	International Political Economy
ITUC	International Trade Union Confederation
ITUCs	Interregional Trade Union Councils
JiT	Just in Time
LDC	Less Developed Countries
MNC	Multi National Corporation
NGO	Non-Governmental Organisation
OECD	Organisation for Economic Co-operation and Development
R&D	Research and Development
SEWA	Self-Employed Women's Association
SiD	Specialarbejderforbundet i Danmark
SMU	Social Movement Unionism

TUC	Trades Union Congress
TGWU	Transport and General Workers Union
TUAC	Trade Union Advisory Committee to the OECD
UN	United Nations
UNICE	Employers' Confederations of Europe
UNISON	The Public Services Union
WCL	World Confederation of Labour
WIEGO	Women in Informal Employment Globalizing and Organizing
WSF	World Social Forum
WTO	World Trade Organisation

PREFACE

The labour movement in Britain and across Europe is facing a critical point in its history. A prolonged period of economic uncertainty and austerity has placed workers on the defensive. The 'gig economy' brings precarious employment for millions, traditional industries are threatened, and Brexit brings the prospect of British de-regulation and economic disaster.

Might Trade Unions, already weakened over decades, be able to provide some resistance and defend the interests of workers? Can these organisations, born in a different era, really be effective in a globalised world that they were never meant to operate in?

To ask such questions is not new. For a generation there have been doubts as to the relevance of Trade Unions in a changing world. This book looks to research from the past to help understand the trajectory the labour movement has been on, and its possible destination. Critically, it highlights how whilst contemporary challenges may seem unique, they are echoes of those faced in the 1980s, 1990s and 2000s. And that potential solutions rejected then, could save the movement in the future.

INTRODUCTION. LABOUR IN THE GLOBAL POLITICAL ECONOMY

A specific focus of this research is the degree to which "social movement unionism" (Moody, 1997, p4) can be seen as a framework for renewal for the modern labour movement. And the extent to which this academic concept has been used by the labour movement in its strategies to respond to the pressures of globalisation.

Social movement unionism describes practices and processes apparently adopted by trade unions that shifted towards their more socially oriented roots (Gallin, 2002) in recent years. In essence, it can be seen as a response on behalf of the labour movement to the pressure of globalisation that is "quite simply the biggest challenge to the free trade union movement in its long struggle on behalf of working men and women around the world" (ICFTU, 1997, p4).

From this starting point analysis moves to the context in which the labour movement operates, and the strategies (either derivative of social movement unionism or not), that have been employed by the various key elements of the movement at the national, regional (European), and global levels.

Social movement unionism is built upon a rejection of the

idea that the labour movement's demise is inevitable. Instead it presents the opportunity for the labour movement to take on "a process of recomposition in most of its key sectors" (Munck, 1998, p6). But social movement unionism's meaning is multifaceted. As with any construct analysed in IPE, it could be seen as a theoretical idea that is meaningless for workers and unions at the ground level of the global political economy. However, for some this form of unionism and its components are seen as concrete goals to be aimed for by the labour movement, resembling at times a prescriptive alternative to existing structures and practices (Waterman, 1998, 2001; Munck, 2002). Be that through increased militancy, growing co-operation with other social movements, or moves to widen participation.

In order to understand this new type of unionism and its potential impacts, this research seeks to analyse and understand key issues that have long affected the modern labour movement. Of critical importance are the intertwined processes of globalisation, specifically the globalisation of production, technology, governance and civil society, all of which combine to present the labour movement with challenges and in some instances opportunities.

From that foundation it is possible to then contextualise

the historic attitudes and arguments of those within labour organisations. It will be argued that the labour movement has already had the opportunity to reach beyond traditional frameworks and to develop new processes and structures akin to those argued for within the social movement unionism debate. But there has been a hesitancy and defensiveness often ignored within academic discussions.

It will also be revealed that organisations such as the Self Employed Women's Association (SEWA) present a long-standing example of how social movement unionist principles are being implemented in strategies of worker protection and resistance against the pressures of the global age. Such organisations are argued to provide a form of testing ground for social movement unionism that traditional labour organisations may be well served to pay close attention to.

Research Methodology

Analysis will take a multi-level perspective, with focus split between the national, European and global levels of action. This multi-level model is a powerful tool as it allows the highlighting of observable trends across divides in socio-politics.

Because of the intertwining and interdependent nature that the national, regional and global levels take, processes and structures present at one level are often replicated or at least can be seen as having a major influence on others.

Such a perspective is exemplified in Gramscian-inspired theory that argues that the global system "structures of authority comprise not one but at least three levels: the macro-regional level, the old state level, and the micro-regional level" (Cox, 1993, p263). Because we are essentially analysing a "complex multi-level world system" (Cox, 1993, p263) in which the levels are interdependent and intertwining, to remove one level of analysis from the others would in turn remove vital components of understanding and context from that analysis.

The UK was chosen as the national level of analysis as its socio-political history presents a clear and sometimes extreme example of the cumulative pressures facing the labour movement. Looking back we can also see a scepticism and reluctance within labour organisations to change that hampered their redevelopment in the past. The result is that trade unions now face Brexit and the next stage of globalisation in a weakened position, in part because of the choices of their own leaders.

The European region was chosen as the second level of

analysis as it is the most politically, socially, and economically developed supranational area in the global political economy. Because of this there is a clear framework of political institutions with which European level labour organisations operate, meaning that any arguments regarding changes in the latter come within a clear and viable socio-political context. The impact of Brexit on these structures is unclear, but they are likely to survive either as an inspiration to British stakeholders or a viable space in which to operate.

A central foundation of this research is the insight gained from a series of historic face-to-face interviews. These were conducted with figures within key British unions, as well as European and international labour organisations over a decade ago. These interviews provide the original insights and arguments of this research, with concerns and attitudes echoing those of today and tomorrow.

Divergent Forms of Labour

It is necessary to understand what the term labour means before discussing its place in the global political economy. Labour can be understood as a twofold concept, on the one hand it is the actual physical performance of work, whilst on the other it is a term that acts as a label for the people who perform this work. Our conceptions of the former element of labour as work in IPE are increasingly challenged by changes within the process and organisation of work (Hyman and Streeck, 1989) that make traditional frameworks of understanding obsolete. These changes have in turn challenged the position in IPE of the second, human element of labour. The understanding of such changes and challenges are central to this research and are discussed in chapter three.

As well as the distinction between work and workers, there is an initial twofold distinction to be made between protected and unprotected labour. Conventionally the term 'protected labour' signifies labour that is organised and defended most often by a trade union (O'Brien, 2000a, p38), presenting a symbolic expression of all labour. Unprotected workers on the other hand are "vulnerable people in forms of work that receive little union, political party, or state protection from those who hold power" (O'Brien, 2000a, p39).

It is important to understand that in the global political economy, with the challenges facing labour, even unionised workers may at times be unprotected. This occurs as union power and leverage has been prised away by market and political forces without an effective response by the labour movement. Both protected and unprotected labour are understood to be important for our understanding of developments within the labour movement in this thesis. Beneath the subsets of protected and unprotected labour, more groupings of workers are to be observed. Workers' age, gender and class add to differing positions within the workplace hierarchy to provide a truly heterogeneous labour force.

To focus simply on a given section of the global workforce such as white males in a particular form of employment is myopic, and instead the term labour is taken to signify all workers. This wide focus is particularly necessary when one realises that in recent years there has been a fracturing of traditional working class identities as various processes have changed the way work is performed. It should be pointed out however, that it is questionable whether the stereotypical working class identity was ever more than an artificial construct. Women for example, have always had a role in the performance of work thought history, so whilst we observe a contemporary "heterogeneous labour force" (Munck, 1998, p7) this has always been the case.

The Importance of Unprotected Workers in the Global Political Economy

Women and other often ignored elements of the global workforce including migrant workers, are important in the development of an effective global labour movement. By recognising the position that these sets of workers hold within the global political economy, this research builds an argument for widening the labour movement agenda in line with Gramscian idea of a social grouping moving beyond its own narrow corporate interests in order that it may build a wider, more inclusive social movement.

Whilst female labour's true importance is highlighted by figures which argue that in the mid-1990s, within the global political economy some "$16 trillion of global output [was] invisible, $11 trillion produced by women" (United Nations Human Development Report, 1995, p97), at times trade unions appear ignorant of the needs of women (shown in later chapters), or their importance for the labour movement. When this ignorance of women is present, labour organisations are overlooking a wide range of tasks that includes home-based work, domestic work and family support work (UNDP, 1998. p8). These tasks are just as important to the social relations of production that form the basis of society, and to ignore their impact on the wider world is to ignore an important social force that could contribute toward the creation of a coherent counter-hegemonic bloc.

Child and migrant labour are also worthy of mention here as their exploitation is "a pervasive problem throughout the world, especially in developing countries" (Siddiqi and Patrinos, 2001, p1), that again appears to be almost forgotten by traditional labour organisations. The importance of children to the global political economy becomes clear when one realises that in the world as far back as 2002 there were at least 250 million working children between the ages of five and fourteen in developing countries[1], with around half of these children estimated to be working what can be described as full-time hours. These 250 million workers produce large output for the global economy, yet with much attention being paid to issues affecting what may described as 'normal' sets of workers, the plight of these workers is often ignored. Despite campaigns such as that of the International Labour Organisation (ILO) to "embark upon a world-wide campaign against child labour"

1. Interview with IGTLWF Official, 11/8/2002.

(Reich, 1996, p 1), other organisations are again apparently ignorant of the potential social power that could be gained through effectively protecting such workers.

In the globalised world, with transport and communication links becoming ever more developed in what has been termed "global shrinkage" (Stalker. 2000, p26), the issue of migration is critical in the study of labour. Legal economic migrants travel the world today seeking work, with many more millions of illegal economic migrants that must be remembered. Often operating in poor jobs with poor conditions, these workers bear the brunt of society's frustration as they are treated as scapegoats for wider societal issues that are not their fault (Harris, 1995, p 187).

The implicit understanding of this research is that were the labour movement as a whole to address the plight of such workers, not only would the new workers bring increased leverage through sheer scale of numbers, but there would also be a widening of horizons for those within the labour movement. This would happen as addressing issues surrounding these workers would be to address a wide range of socio-political dynamics including cultural differences, environmental issues, governmental policies, multi-culturalism, and the importance of the informal economy in which these people are so often found working. Such a process would undoubtedly lead to the labour movement coming into contact with other social movements, easing a shift in organisation and action towards that of social movement unionism.

Within the formal economy that the labour movement operates and pays most attention to, there is an increasing trend towards change in work that results in less full-time, secure employment (Rifkin, 1995), as discussed in chapter three. This subsequently means a shift towards insecure, often part-time, contract or shift work, and the workers within these growing 'sectors' present a large grouping of actors often excluded from the labour movement. It is within the informal sector of the global political economy that holds no rights or protections for those working within it, that much unprotected labour finds itself positioned (WIEGO, 2003a).

These workers represent a huge body of untapped potential for the labour movement, which could dramatically increase the movement's power and legitimacy if only by force of numbers[2]. Yet it may be the case that some of these workers

---

2. Interview with ETUC Official, 22 17/2002.

neither need nor want to be brought into the framework created by the traditional western model labour movement. At present there is a dynamic self-organisation movement especially amongst women around the world that has developed in the absence of traditional trade unions. Such organisations, analysed in chapter six, are argued to represent a true development of social movement unionism. In this sense they provide the labour movement with a test scenario for social movement unionism that will show whether this is a framework for action capable of reinvigorating existing organisations.

There are certain elements of the labour movement who have felt that these excluded sections of the workforce are important to their future, an apparent example being the ICFTU that stated many years ago that "organising workers in the informal economy has become a vital necessity for the future of the trade union movement" (ICFTU, 2001b, p1). Yet many other figures and organisations in the labour movement as a whole have argued that "the informal sector is a transitory phenomenon" (Gallin, 2001, p531) that will be naturally subsumed into the organised element of labour, a standpoint that legitimises a rejection of calls to widen union activities and focuses to incorporate excluded workers.

Such a process of workforce re-composition seems unlikely however, as unprotected, cheap and mobile workers perfectly suit many economic needs in the current global age. In turn it seems natural that capital as a collective body will attempt to retain their use. The labour movement must acknowledge the importance that millions of unprotected workers would have for its influence, as well as the broadening of the issues it would address. With the "stabilisation of the formal sector...depend[ing] on the organisation of the informal sector" (ILO, 1999, p2) it appears that a widening of participation for the labour movement "serves the interests of the majority of workers world-wide" (Gallin, 2001, p532).

Structure of the book

The next chapter presents a Gramscian inspired theoretical framework upon which the research rests, and will also discuss the central elements of social movement unionism that are taken as being key for the future development of the labour movement. Gramscian theory is used in this research as it allows for analysis of the political economy without imposing a narrow focus on political and economic structures and actors. Instead, social forces and agents, such as workers and the labour movement, are seen as having the potential to influence their environment and respond to challenges faced. This chapter will give the findings and arguments of this thesis a solid foundation upon which to rest, meaning that context and understanding is given.

Chapter three will move to a discussion of the challenges and opportunities that are presented to the labour movement in the modern world. Specifically, there will be analysis of four key processes of globalisation, namely the globalisation of production, globalisation of technology, globalisation of governance and the globalisation of civil society. In doing so it will be argued that whilst there is a process of change occurring in and around the world of work, intertwined processes also provide labour with opportunities to redevelop their ways of operating and organising. This is central to the research as it provides a detailed overview of the context within which the labour movement now operates. By exploring the challenges and opportunities presented to the labour movement, it will be possible to more fully understand to what extent any developments within the labour movement are actually aimed at responding to them, and to what extent the strategies pursued are realistic or successful.

Chapter four shifts to analysis of tangible developments.

Here the experiences of the British labour movement will be analysed, with attention being focused on developments from 1979 to the present day. This period represents the key challenges posed by globalisation to the labour movement, across all levels of analysis. There will be a discussion of whether the British labour movement has previously succeeded in addressing the challenges faced, and whether social movement unionism has been embraced by the labour movement at this level as a model for changing organisation and action. Because of the stark conditions within which the labour movement has found itself operating in Britain, this national framework for analysis represents a good context within which to understand how the labour movement has attempted to 'fight back'. It will be asked to what extent the labour movement has pursued a dynamic and coordinated process of renewal, and whether action at the national level is enough in the globalised age.

Chapter five will move the focus upwards so the European regional level of the labour movement is analysed. Specifically there will be discussion of three key dimensions, namely the centralised European level presented by the ETUC, the industry level of the International Trade Confederations (ITCs), and company level of action where European Works Councils (EWCs) play an important role. It will be asked whether conditions necessary for the successful internationalisation of the labour movement integral in a modern form of social movement unionism are in place or are being enacted upon. The need for ground level popular support, a lack of reliance on political institutions and the presence of a viable social opponent will be shown to be important prerequisites for internationalisation that are at present missing. This regional level is important for this research as it presents a pivotal dimension of socio-political action, linking national actors and policies to the more overarching global arena. Any successful redevelopment of the labour movement at this level may point towards processes that have important ramifications for workers at national levels.

Chapter Six analyses the global dimension of the labour movement, exploring if the peak level of the labour movement is driving forward moves towards social movement unionism. It will be asked whether, given the globalising of civil society and the importance of social movements, this global dimension of the labour movement is capable in its current form of presenting a united framework for the representation of workers. Given a discussion of the importance of the informal economy in the modern global political economy, and the pivotal role that women often play in this dimension of the global political economy, there are at present a number of women-led organisations that point towards a true social movement unionism. The self-organising principles and a reliance on fluid and dynamic processes that inform these organisations will be argued to be more applicable to the lives of workers than the traditional institutional processes and structures held by the traditional western model labour movement.

It will be argued that a social forum model at the global level holds the potential to allow the organic development of linkages between the labour movement and other social movements. In turn such a process could herald a move towards a repositioning of the labour movement as a societal actor more suited to the modern global political economy, and the social led form of action favoured by women's groups. These women's groups serve to test social movement unionism as they are utilising its main elements in a fashion that those in the more traditional labour movement have argued is neither necessarily desirable or indeed practical, in turn testing this thesis' question of whether social movement unionism is a suitable course of development for the modern labour movement.

To conclude chapter seven draws out the recurring themes

highlighted in earlier chapters regarding the apparent rejection on behalf of those within the labour movement of social movement unionism. By showing the manner in which attitudes within the labour movement towards social movement unionism have been at times hostile and negative, and the fashion in which various structural issues cause fracture between labour organisations, it will become explicit that the social movement unionism discussed in academia and explored in chapter two does not match with tangible developments in the labour movement.

Two particular sets of implications will then be explored, namely those surrounding theory and concepts used in discussions of labour in the global political economy, and more practical concerns regarding the dynamic between labour organisations and social movements. It will be argued that the findings of this research have highlighted the need to question the theoretical conception of plurality and diversity within civil society, the very meaning that the term labour is taken to hold, and has also shown the explicit need to discuss issues of governance and action as being multi- dimensional and not confined to a single level of analysis. Specifically regarding the dynamics between labour organisations and social movements, it will be shown that this research has highlighted tensions caused by the self-portrayal of unions. It is also argued that campaigns and objectives undertaken by unions do not fit with social movement unionist principles. A final point to be presented is that an increased understanding of the role new forms of labour organisation and social forums play in the global political economy is necessary if future research is to fully understand the possibilities for redevelopment for the traditional labour movement.

1. GRAMSCIAN THOUGHT AND SOCIAL MOVEMENT UNIONISM IN THE STUDY OF LABOUR

Introduction

This chapter provides the theoretical framework and context upon which this research rests. There will be a detailed discussion of the central concepts of Gramscian thought that are relevant to the discussion of labour, namely hegemony and the interrelated concepts of counter hegemony, social forces and civil society. These theoretical constructs allow an understanding of the contemporary political economy that looks beyond merely the political and economic, to instead show the importance of social forces and actors. There will be analysis of neo-Gramscian application of these concepts, specifically focusing on the work of Cox in understanding hegemony and potential change at the global level of the political economy. Following a section on the criticisms levelled at the application of Gramscian thought in the contemporary age, there will also be a discussion of the significance of this body of thought for the study of labour within IPE.

Building alliances in a bid to create a historic bloc capable of attaining hegemony (Gramsci, 1971) is central to Gramscian though. As a key element of this process for the contemporary labour movement would involve interaction with social movements, the second substantive section of this chapter moves to discuss social movements and their defining properties. These social actors provide the basis for social movement unionism taken here as a template for organising and operating suited to the modern age. It will be argued that precisely because these organisations are movements, and not necessarily institutionalised, confusion as to their defining traits must be overcome. Central features will be identified however, so that it may be argued for the purposes of this thesis, that social movements are seen to be associations of people with most commonly, but not always, a goal of influencing the political economy.

Building upon this understanding of what a social movement may be seen as, the following section will then analyse social movement unionism. This term is taken to represent the new forms of organising for the labour movement in the modern political economy. Three central dimensions of this form of unionism will be explored, namely internal changes to the way the labour movement operates, a growing emphasis on internationalisation, and increased linkages to other social movements within civil society. The importance of these changes in labour movement practices will be analysed. In particular, the focus will rest on issues such as potential problems of labour organisations' compatibility with other social movements, attitudes towards 'new' forms of operating, and the exclusion of less organised elements of society from social movement unionism.

Hegemony, Civil Society and Social Forces in the Study of Labour

The claims made by contemporary IPE theorists to a social movement unionism draw implicitly upon key elements of Gramscian thought. These central themes will be discussed here: hegemony, counter-hegemony, civil society and social forces. These were initially developed in a bid to step away from the mechanical determinism of classical Marxism that promoted "the passive attitude of waiting for the inevitable economic collapse [that] discouraged the exercise of political initiatives by the labour movement" (Simon, 1991, p14). Instead of this, Gramsci developed a more critical, societal focused theoretical framework in order that the failures of socialism in challenging national hegemonies around the world were better understood.

Remaining firmly rooted in an understanding of the importance of the working class and their place within society, Gramsci argued that the production structure within which they operated was central to theoretical and real world understandings. Understanding that hegemony must to a great extent "necessarily be based on the decisive function exercised by the leading group in the decisive nucleus of economic activity" (Gramsci, 1971, p 161), he shifted away from economic determinism by analysing how social relations and forces stemming from positions within production were central to life. Indeed he was able to argue forcibly that social relations across all aspects of the political and social "interpenetrate with the relations of production" (Simon, 1991, p28).

This concept of hegemony is the central point for any discussion of Gramscian theory, as Gramsci was concerned with not only how the working class may challenge hegemonic orders, but also how the "apparatus or mechanisms of hegemony of the dominant class" (Cox, 1983, p163) were built and maintained. Critically, hegemony for the Gramscian is not simply the "domination by means of force, but of consent by means of political and ideological leadership" (Simon, 1982, p21), meaning that one must acknowledge and understand much more than mere physical domination. Instead we are led to acknowledge the social forces and relations inherent within the intertwining conceptualisations of civil and political society, which form the state within a historic bloc.

For Gramsci, it is not enough that a particular grouping attempts to seize hegemony through the simple articulation of their economic desires, or through means of force alone. Whilst at certain times a short and forceful "war of movement" (Simon, 1982, p24) may be enough to seize control of a particularly one dimensional form of state such as was the case in the Russian revolution of 1917, more often a longer, more careful strategy is necessary. This is known as the "war of position" (Gramsci, 1971, p238), and involves the gradual building up of the societal foundations of a new state. Inherent in this gradual shift towards a hegemonic position is the move towards gaining the "consent of other classes and social forces through creating and maintaining a system of alliances by means of political and ideological struggle" (Simon, 1991, p23-24), a process that will lead to a new hegemonic order.

In order that this movement is achieved, the class aiming at achieving hegemony must shift its focus beyond its "own corporate interests...[and] transcend the corporate limits of the purely economic class, and can and must become the interests of other subordinate groups too" (Gramsci, 1971, pp 181-2). This signifies a move towards a more socio-political phase of operating for a class or grouping, which holds central to it an understanding of the importance of social relations in the quest for hegemony. Only when a group opens itself up to the importance of other democratic struggles, and attempts to gain "leadership of these democratic, non-class aspirations of the people" (Simon, 1982, p45) can the move towards counter-hegemony truly begin.

This is a creation of essentially a coalition of social forces and classes, that will involve the unification by the working class of "popular-democratic struggles with its own...so as to build up a national-popular collective will" (Simon, 1982, p45), essentially forming a cohesive revolutionary movement capable of providing true counter-hegemony. The war of position which this is integral to, is seen as being won in a more decisive and definitive fashion (Gramsci, 1971, p239) than the more overt and immediate struggles of a war of movement, the last of which for Gramsci's was "the events of 1917" (Gramsci, 1971, p235).

That it is not enough to simply take command of institutions through force in the search for hegemony points to a central Gramscian concept, namely the "extended, or integral, concept of the state" (Showstack Sassoon, 1987, p109). Gramsci himself argued that "little understanding of the state means little class consciousness; hence low level of effectiveness" (Gramsci, 1971, p275), so understanding of hegemony must necessarily involve an understanding of the state as much as the moves towards social cohesion. Utilising the term "integral state" (Simon, 1982, p81), Gramsci identifies a configuration that is "the entire complex of practical and theoretical; activities with which the ruling class not only maintains its dominance but manages to win the consent of those over whom it rules" (Gramsci, 1971, p244), or more succinctly the "hegemony protected by the armour of coercion" (Gramsci, 1971, p262).

Within the state we see the relatively overt institutions of hegemony, be they government, police, armed forces, but so as not to demonise the state itself as it holds more educative and cultural aspects too, the term political society is used to denote the coercive relations within the state apparatus. These apparatus that counter-hegemonic groups wish to attain control of, are complemented by institutions and frameworks known as "civil society" (Gramsci, 1971, p12), a societal complement so political society.

For Gramsci, the integral state is not an abstract concept, but rather incorporates political society mentioned above, and a civil society that "is the ensemble of organisms commonly called private" (Gramsci, 1971, p12). This civil society includes all the organisations and institutions such as churches, political parties, trade unions, and other societal groupings that are "distinct from the process of production and from the coercive apparatuses of the state" (Simon, 1982, p69). It is within civil society where both political and ideological positions are formed and struggles take place. Importantly for Gramscians, it is not only economic focused class struggles that are to be found here, but also "all popular-democratic struggles which arise out of the different ways in which people are grouped together" (Simon, 1982, p69). The final form of state is created by the culmination of both this civil society and the political society mentioned above.

By looking at the social relations of production, political and civil society, and the resultant formations of the state, Gramsci moves to present the all-encompassing concept of a historic bloc. This historic bloc is "the site of the joining together of two levels of analysis, the theoretical and the second concrete in the description of the linking of these two areas [structure and superstructure] in real society" (Showstack Sassoon, 1987, p121).

This concept provides us with an overview of the formations and social relations of a given period in time of a particular nation, and the goal of a group wishing to attain hegemony is to create an alternative, or counter-hegemonic bloc. "The construction of a historic bloc is a precondition for the exercise of hegemony" (Rupert, 1993, p80), as it involves the interrelated processes of political, economic and cultural changes brought about through struggles within civil society and the social relations of production. When a particular class or grouping attains leadership of a coalition of social forces within civil society, as well as leadership within the sphere of production, it may be said to have formed a historic bloc, signifying a point at which hegemony may then be gained.

Because of the culmination of processes involved in creating a historic bloc, it is entirely conceivable that differing state formations or social relations will exist at varying times within the same historic bloc. This highlights the effort, co-ordination and commitment that is required to effectively challenge existing hegemony at a given moment in Gramsci's theoretical conception.

Gramsci's ideas provide a uniquely societal focused understanding of the world around us. The primacy of the economic production structure is acknowledged without a mechanistic perspective that relies merely on the political and economic for understanding. Instead social forces and relations are brought into analysis, with the conjuncture of social relations within production, civil society, political society, and the resultant war of position building to the attainment and maintenance of hegemony within the political economy.

This theoretical framework was developed in a particular era, with the goal of analysing "the consequences of specific political forms, the potential of the working class to develop a strategy to modify the forms of domination in capitalist society, and the problems of constructing a socialist state with a wide social basis" (Showstack Sassoon, 1987, p 17). He attempted to understand real world developments in the early 20th century, with economism failing to lead to effective socialism around the world. With this context in mind, it is perhaps debatable whether this framework emphasising "the national dimension" (Showstack Sassoon, 1987, p20 1), is applicable to the modern era.

Neo-Gramscian Thought in the Global Age

In recent years theorists have taken the central concepts of Gramscian thought and used them in analysis of the modern world. Most central of these theorists is Robert Cox, who from the early 1980s developed what has been termed a Neo-Gramscian framework of understanding. Cox's work signifies a rejection of mainstream positivist IPE that found difficulty in explaining or understanding substantive changes to the world order in the 1970s and 80s (Bieler and Morton, 2004b), and instead represents a move to understand how existing world orders have come into being, and how the norms, institutions and practices have emerged, with specific focus on "what forces may have the emancipatory potential to change or transform the prevailing order" (Bieler and Morton, 2004a, p87).

In doing so, Cox used the Gramscian understanding of hegemony with its intertwined concepts of historic blocs, social relations, political and civil society, to understand change in the global political economy by giving "proper attention to social forces and processes" (Cox, 1981, p 128). For Cox, hegemony in the global age is not simply a realist domination of states through force or power, it is instead based on a "fit between a configuration of material power, the prevalent collective image of world order and a set of institutions which administer the order with a certain semblance of universality" (Cox, 1981, p139). Essentially Cox is striving to analyse "a larger picture of the whole of which the initially contemplated part is just one component, and seeks to understand the processes of change" (Cox, 1981, p129) therein.

Whereas Gramsci discussed hegemony as being constructed through social relations within civil and political society, leading to an almost consensual hegemony, Cox moves the discussion onwards to talk of hegemony being constituted within a particular historical structure through three spheres of activity, incorporating both the national and international levels of analysis. These are the "social relations of production" (Cox, 1987, p 11) that are the point of departure for the analysis of hegemony; "forms of state as derived from a study of state/society complexes" (Cox, 1981, p 138); and finally "world orders, i.e. the particular configurations of forces which successively define the problematic or war and peace for the ensemble of states" (Cox, 1981, p138). Cox argued that changes within any one of these spheres could lead to significant changes in the others, due to the interrelated and reinforcing nature that they take (Rupert, 1995).

The significance of the social relations of production is

central, as by analysing differing modes of social relations of production, one can "question what promotes the emergence of particular modes and what might explain how modes combine or undergo transformation" (Bieler and Morton, 2004a, p89; Cox, 1987, p103). Essentially we are led to understand how dynamics within social relations of production can give rise to differing social forces that may in turn provide the basis for forms of state. This is possible as the state is not a given, but can rather take various forms, constituted by political and civil society as posited by Gramsci. Changes in the form of the state can in turn help shape forms of a world order that is constructed through social relations, political and civil society. And just as importantly we are shown that such power dynamics are not simply linear, and can instead reverse.

Within these spheres of activity, three interrelated forces are found, namely "material capabilities [which] are productive and destructive forces" (Cox, 1981, p136), "ideas" (Cox, 1981, p136), and "institutions" (Cox, 1981, p136) that are in effect a combination of the former two. Again these three elements of society have an interrelated form that means that changes in one can affect the other two in various manners. By taking these sets of forces and activity, Cox argued that shifts towards hegemony and in turn the hegemonic order, can be understood. Critically however, Cox took this model of analysis and moved beyond the spatial boundaries of the nation state in a fashion not explicitly tried by Gramsci, for Cox has endeavoured to explain periods of change and hegemony at the global level, in order that prospects for change in the future are highlighted (Gill, 1993, p4).

This Neo Gramscian work uses the concepts of social relations within production as well as forms of state and world order, to analyse the hegemonic formations of historic periods and structures. In doing so it is argued that global hegemony, just as national hegemony in the Gramscian understanding, cann ot come from mere domination, but instead also rests upon social relations and forces within "global civil society" (Cox, 1983, p 171). This shifts our focus away from inter-state relations as seen in neo-realism towards a more societal focused perspective that holds social relations as key at all levels of analysis. Looking towards the global level, Cox remains aware of the nation state, arguing that periods of global hegemony stem from a particular national hegemonic bloc, "projected outwards on a world scale" (Bieler and Morton, 2004a, p87). In other words, global hegemony rests upon national hegemony that can expand beyond a particular social order to move outward on a world scale through the international expansion of a particular form of social relations of production (Cox, 1987, pp149-50; 1983, p171).

Just as Gramsci's concept of hegemony allowed for understanding of the attainment and maintenance of hegemony at the national level, so here we are allowed to understand the possibility for change at the global level. Rather than relying on analysing international institutions that can be seen as supporting the "internationalisation of Gramsci's extended state" (Rupert, 1993, p88) and the prospect for attaining change though those, Cox is careful to retain a focus at the national level as much as the global. This is because in real terms the national level is seen as the only dimension wherein a counter-hegemonic historic bloc can truly be formed, due to the need for a war of position involving "the building up [of] the socio-political base for change" Cox, 1983, pp 173-4). For whilst there is debate surrounding the "internationalising of the state and civil society" (Gill, 1993, p4), these still rest upon the national dimension for support. Essentially we are being told of the importance of not simply relying on one level of analysis for our insights, and instead of the continued importance even in the global age of the state, as "hegemony can therefore operate at two levels" (Bieler and Morton, 2004a, p93), meaning that resistance and change as well as analysis can in tum involve both levels in a similar fashion.

Towards a Critical Perspective of Gramscian Thought

The concepts discussed above have not been applied to modern IPE without critique, and this section will outline some of the key concerns raised with regards to a Gramscian inspired analysis of IPE. Amongst these "substantial doubts" (Germain and Kenny, 1998, p4) raised over the employment of Gramscian thought in contemporary IPE is the issue of exclusivity, for whilst Gramscian thought presents a socially focused theoretical framework, there are times when elites and organised elements of society obtain much of the focus (Drainville, 1994) to the exclusion of less visible societal elements (Germain and Kenny, 1998). Whilst it is true that Gramsci's thought focused on organised class groupings, there is no reason that contemporary theorisation cannot take this into account and attempt to remedy it.

With this in mind this research explicitly acknowledges the need to look beyond traditional identities surrounding what can be seen as male organised workers, and will bring less organised elements of society into the focus. It will be argued that women in particular hold great insights for societal change in IPE, due to the path of resistance and social agency they have followed in certain cases that moves away from the traditional elite, top-down approach to one more aware of the "contextual nature of resistance" (Marchand and Runyan, 2000, p 19). In doing so they have shown the potential for societal resistance that steps beyond formal and institutionalised bodies, bringing as they do a recognition that social groupings within civil society that can bring dynamic forms of organising and understanding to discussions of IPE (Runyan, 1997).

The second criticism of Gramscian thought regards whether Gramsci's "key concepts can be internationalised in quite a way that the new Gramscians propose" (Germain and Kenny, 1998, p4), in turn raising doubts over whether this is a theoretical framework suitable for the 'globalised' 21st century. The problematic stems from the fact that Gramsci's theory focused on the national level of analysis, discussing in detail structures, forces and change within the extended state analysed above. To blindly transplant Gramsci's thought to the global age without any forethought would no doubt risk nullifying any insights gained, but that is not what neo-Gramscians led by Cox have attempted to do. Instead there has been recognition of the importance of hegemony built not on coercion but also by co-opting and social forces, both at the national and international level.

When looking at socio-political issues in the early 20th century, Gramsci could not have envisaged the internationalisation of production and the state that has occurred in recent years (Cox, 1983), and due to this he could not have designed his theoretical framework to suit the future. He did however, pay attention to the question of international relations, arguing "the line of development is towards internationalism, but the point of departure is national" (Gramsci, 1971, p240). Essentially Gramsci recognised the international level of analysis was important, and linked to the social relations that stem from the national level. Cox's work represents an attempt to carry this perspective forward by developing the concepts discussed above, in a manner that allows insights explicitly regarding the global level to be made. It is pure conjecture whether Gramsci would have wished this to be done, or would have done it himself, but it is the theorists place to adapt conceptual tools of the past rather than abandoning useful tools of enquiry, particularly as for Gramsci, "transformative praxis need not stop at the border of the state" (Rupert, 1993, p87). Indeed as Gramsci stated, all relations of hegemony are within "the international and world-wide field, between complexes of national and continental citizens" (Gramsci, 1978, p350), so "the demand to return Gramsci to his historical context need not prevent the possibility of approaching ideas both in and beyond their context" (Bieler and Morton, 2004a, p 104).

This question of globalising tendencies leads to another criticism, particularly of neo-Gramscian work, namely the role of the state in analysis. Some commentators such as Burnham (1991) have argued that "neo-Gramscian approach to the world order seeks to replace state centred frameworks with a study of class forces" (Burnham, 1991, p86), a comment that holds implicit a criticism that the state is therefore somehow ignored. It is argued that too much emphasis is placed on the role of ideology in explaining socio-political change and policy formation in the modern age (Burnham, 1991), but this and the previous criticism overlooks the strong position of the state in both Gramscian and neo-Gramscian arguments. As has been shown above, both theorisations hold the role of the state as critical in the development of hegemony at the dual levels of nation state and internationally. It was shown explicitly that for neo-Gramscian thought, discussions of hegemony depart from the state, and that hegemony is spread across the globe though a diffusion of social relations, political formations and institutionalisation (Cox, 1981,

1983, 1987). This is in fact a similar position to Burnham's when he argues that it is "a fallacy to suppose that the importance of the nation state has diminished with the rapid internationalisation of capital" (Burnham, 1991, p86), and does not "render a theory of the state redundant" (Burnham, 1991, p88).

Another argument regarding neo-Gramscian thought is that its account of power relations is too top down, with the state seen more as a part of a conveyer belt of power relations from "the global to the national within the internationalisation of the state" (Bieler and Morton, 2004a, p 101; Panitch et al. 2000). This points to an argument again that states are overlooked or somehow seen as powerless, this time in terms of their place in orchestrating globalisation, or in other terms being agents for globalisation. But again, one must point to the fact that neo-Gramscian theory acknowledges a dual dimension to changes in world order, namely that changes in any of the three main structures, namely the state, relations of production or the world order, can bring about change in the others. Thus there is an inherent recognition of reciprocity within IPE brought by neo-Gramscian work including Cox's analysis of IPE (Cox, 1981, 1983, 1987).

Implications of Gramscian Inspired Theory for the Study of Labour in IPE

The central concepts of Gramscian thought and how they have been adapted for analysis in the contemporary global world have direct implications for the study of labour in IPE. By moving away from a purely economic or politically focused frame of reference towards a framework that is built upon the power of social relations and forces, we are in a position to understand the role that labour plays in the modern world and the potential that exists for the labour movement to move towards changing the order around it. Of central importance is the fundamental understanding that social relations and forces are critical in producing particular socio-political formations, thus the power of social agents to effect change on the world around them should not be underestimated. Even in a time when labour has been placed on the defensive by the pressures of globalisation, there is still an inherent possibility that this social grouping may bring about hegemonic change, or at least challenge conceptions held across the world.

The understanding of the state as incorporating not only the political but also the more societal civil society is important for this potential change, as it provides a space in which the labour movement operates free of direct influence from political apparatuses. This battleground is where the labour movement will embark upon a "war of position" (Gramsci, 1971, p238) in a bid to challenge the hegemonic order that has placed it on the defensive in recent years.

Indeed an upsurge in the number of strikes across the world in recent years may indicate that such a struggle is at least beginning to take place (Moody, 1997). But the Gramscian perspective on the requirements to build a counter-hegemonic consensus can be seen to hold the biggest implication for studying labour, as it is argued that a reliance on a groups defined "corporate interests" (Gramsci, 1971, p 181) is not enough to build a historic bloc capable of gaining hegemony or challenging the prevailing order. Instead it is imperative that the labour movement develops its outlook to that of a wider scale, in doing so taking "account of the interests of other classes and social forces and find ways of combining them with its own interests" (Simon, 1991, p24). Such a move if successful, or indeed if actually attempted would lead to the development of a coalition of social forces (Munck, 1998) with sufficient leverage and influence to effectively bring about change in the prevailing political economy. Such a move on behalf of the labour movement could result not only in changes regarding the structures and practices internal to it, but also changes in attitudes and beliefs as increased interaction with other movements has effect.

The structures within which networks of "alliances with social movements" (Simon, 1991, p46) are developed are also important. For the Gramscian concepts discussed here, and the Neo-Gramscian thought thereafter, point us towards the prevailing importance of traditional structures even in the global age. For whilst international institutions such as the UN or the European Union (EU) may appear to point towards an internationalisation of governance that would shift the focus of attention for the labour movement, we are reminded of a different reality. This reality is that even today the nation state is an important area of contestation, as socio-political change may be brought about across the globe as much from social relations stemming from the national level, as from the global (Cox, 1983, p169). Whilst a policy of attempting to influence "the mechanisms of international organisation" (Bieler and Morton, 2004, p93) is important in the actions of the modern labour movement, this is not enough.

A balance must be sought, between the need for movements of resistance and change to "draw sufficient support in the world system" (Cox, 1993, p273), and to build and maintain support within national spaces. It is perhaps important that inherently international organisations such as the International Confederation of Free Trade Unions (ICFTU) play a role in these processes, potentially allowing a truly balanced and multilevel approach to hegemonic change to be pursued, but their power is built upon the creation of a strong labour movement based at the national level.

The essential importance of Gramscian inspired theory for the study of labour in the IPE is the fact that it allows for the consideration of questions of resistance to the world order. Looking at the global age, one can ascertain how the changing forms and relations of production, specifically towards a global variant as implicit in the processes of globalisation, may lead to a re-composition of state and civil society relations. In turn, it is possible to ask what new forms of exploitation may exist within the global political economy, and what related modes of resistance and struggle may be observed. Doing so whilst maintaining a theoretical grounding that links back to concepts of hegemony and the related structures and processes, means that important societal issues are addressed without bypassing or ignoring "issues of inequality and exploitation within a political economy" (Bieler and Morton, 2004b, p4).

It is such an avenue of analysis that this research will follow. Bearing in mind the continued call for a challenge to the hegemonic order through the building of alliances with other social groups, the following section will analyse the groupings that the contemporary labour movement could interact with. Specifically there will be analysis of what is meant by the term social movement, and what this means in the real world of socio-politics, as the labour movement will have to extend its focus beyond the economic towards more divergent social issues and groups if a truly counter-hegemonic bloc is to be created.

Social Movements

This research analyses the central developments regarding the labour movement within the modern global political economy using a Gramscian informed approach. A key assertion examined is that for trade unions to effectively operate in contemporary socio-politics, they should draw inspiration from "social movements" (Munck, 1998, pl) that operate across many different issue areas in the modern world, as these movements are more suited to the globalised age, a conception that follows from the Gramscian theory of social linkages discussed above. Whilst this is an easy assertion to make, it is first necessary to understand just what exactly a social movement is, in order that progress may be made. Yet a definition of a social movement is hard to attain, perhaps precisely due to the vagueness of the term 'movement'. Rather than understanding the term to describe a somewhat ethereal form of campaign or undertaking, this research takes a common sense understanding that a movement may be seen as a body of persons with a common objective. With the term social attached, the focus of attention may simply be seen as a grouping of people, with the common aim of influencing a particular aspect of societal life. Yet the membership of, and issues addressed by a movement may change in time, dynamics that give rise to their fluid and apparently loose nature.

Yet when one attempts to gain more in depth understanding of what a social movement is, the elusiveness of the term's central meaning becomes more apparent. One attempt at categorisation has stated a social movement is "a sustained and purposeful collective mobilisation by an identifiable, self-organised group in confrontation with specific power structures, and in the pursuit of socio- economic and political change" (Colas, 2002, p67).

This attempt at definition is successful in narrowing our focus towards 'true' social movements, but is also problematic as further specifics of the definition listed as "secularism ...open membership ...universalism ...[and] publicity" (Colas, 2002, pp72-73) narrow the conception too much.

This research does not begin from an exclusive standpoint that social movements are sustained for any particular period of time, however. For on closer analysis there appears a plethora of single issue, short-term movements that organically grow and then disperse when an issue has been fought, hence a definition as a sustained mobilisation alienates many societal actors and forces. Secondly, claims of secularism, open membership and universalism appear ill-judged attempts to provide what is essentially a westernised definition and understanding of social movements that ignores conceptualisations and formations that may exist in other areas of the world, such as local religious groups specific to a particular area (Walker, 1994; Cox, 1999).

It is perhaps more useful if the fact that the multifaceted nature of social movements actually hampers compartmentalisation is acknowledged, and an understanding of 'common virtues' rather than a rigid, blanket definition is sought. Social movements that compose much of civil society are not necessarily singular or homogenous units, and a comprehensive understanding of modern socio-politics should acknowledge this. What we can be sure of, however, is that these movements are social in nature, a coming together of people for a particular purpose in a space theoretically set outside the domination of political and economic agents. But the 'movement' dimension of social movements causes problems of understanding and definition, as this conception means they are "explicitly at odds with the spatial framing of all ontological possibilities" (Walker, 1994, p673). Thus we are forced to challenge our own theoretical understandings and concepts, in order that more dynamic and applicable conceptualisations are possible.

Instead of relying on traditional ideas of institutional actors operating in defined boundaries, it must be understood that within the modern global political economy there exists a form of social actor that "cannot be pinned down" (Walker, 1994, p677) in the same way as states and economic institutions. Social movements are instead "unbounded, fluid and mobile" (Amoore and Langley, 2004, P 103) in a fashion that means their very membership, form and scope that shape them, are contested. But this is not necessarily a weakness, as such fluidity can be seen as heightening the transformative potential of social movements as they are able to develop and respond to issues and changes in the socio-political arena in which they operate, something that maintains their relevancy and ability to act. Yet this fluidity does not necessarily necessitate a rejection of the concept of a common purpose for those within a movement, for without a goal it is questionable whether they would be significant actors in the modern political economy.

A common understanding of what constitutes a social movement is the relatively traditional Non-Governmental Organisations (NGO) that are "playing a further essential role in international governance" (Murphy, 2000, p795). Often seen in institutional forms, such as organised charities, these visible and limited conceptualisations do not represent all social movements. Instead various grassroots, local, single issue and temporary associations must be brought into the fold, but to do so challenges attempts to build the case for a transformative global civil society. Unity and commonality of vision are both traditionally central to sustained challenges to the hegemonic order (Cox, 1999, p26), yet given the fluidity and dynamism displayed by social movements, these are hard to maintain in the modern world. With these conceptualisations in mind, this research takes the term social movement to represent an often fluid, mobile and dynamic form of social association of people with most commonly, but not exclusively a goal of influencing or impacting upon particular facets of the global political economy. As such the influence of these social groupings on the labour movement will be to challenge a reliance on traditional, institutionalised structures and practices in order that social movement unionism may be effectively pursued. The section that follows will develop arguments presented in chapter one to explore just what exactly is meant by social movement unionism in this research.

Social Movement Unionism

It has been argued that in attempting to respond to contemporary challenges in the political economy, trade unions should become more like these social movements (Munck, 1998, p 1). Social movement unionism is built upon this understanding, with (for the purposes of this research) the term taken to mean a progressive, real world shift back towards the social roots of the labour movement and away from institutionalised, rigid structures and practices. Whilst there is no explicitly clear theoretical framework for social movement unionism, it tends to implicitly follow from Gramscian thought. It is particularly influenced by the Gramscian conceptions of hegemony, counter-hegemony and the social relations and forces therein in its strategy for challenging the current world order.

An understanding of the term social movements as given above assists the identification and analysis of central themes that exist in IPE debate and real world action. Indeed it is defining elements of social movements such as fluidity and dynamism present in social movements, which are precisely the foundations upon which 'new' social movement unions will be built. For social movement unionism comes in the context of calls that in order to remain effective the labour movement must embark upon a "new political discourse that will appeal to a critical mass of workers, labour activists and activists from other issue areas" (Stevis and Boswell, 1997, p96). Rather than focussing on the pursuit of narrow agendas, those who contribute to the social movement union debate argue that the labour movement can operate effectively within global civil society within a wider grouping of social forces challenging the current hegemonic order, much as Gramsci argued for in discussions of a class moving beyond its narrow corporate concerns.

Through analysis of the literature surrounding social movement unionism, including work from O'Brien et al eds. (2000),

Waterman (1998, 2001), Munck (1998, 2002) and Moody (1997), this thesis identifies three key elements in a shift towards social movement unionism that may or may not be seen as being undertaken in the labour movement today. The first of these are moves to change the structures and practices of the labour movement; second is a push towards an explicitly international scope and focus for the labour movement; and third is a development of meaningful linkages to other social movements.

The first of these elements regards the developing of new attitudes and forms of organisation within the labour movement as a whole (Moody, 1997), and is of fundamental importance in the fashion in which it addresses the central tenets of the labour movement, declaring them unfit for the modern world and in need of urgent change (Mcilroy, 2000). Key here is the shift in attitude of the movement and how it addresses its relationship to a wider world politics, away from partnerships towards a more dynamic and militant stance, yet falling short of an explicit "war of movement" (Simon, 1982, p24) as seen by Gramsci. It is arguable that the pursuit of such a policy may present the labour movement as a more vocal and visible representative of workers pushed to the margins of society by capital, meaning its representativeness and effectiveness is increased.

That the labour movement may fight back against capital is not merely theoretical however, and in recent years labour has at times observably reasserted its right to use militant action such as strikes to promote its view point and attempt to gain its demands. An example is that in 1997, labour fought back with massive strikes in Korea with 630,000 workers being on strike, whilst "just before and during mass general strikes were held in Greece, Italy, Spain, Belgium and Ecuador" (Moody, 1997, p14). By doing this, the labour movement mobilised the human agency and resulting social force that lies at its core to fulfil its needs, rather than relying on corporate partnerships that in recent years have been part of relatively unsuccessful plans (Ferner and Hyman eds. 1992) in national arenas such as Britain.

In this respect social movement unionism is built upon an understanding of the importance of social relations within production, as well as civil and political society - showing that a mobilisation of such forces can change the order of the global political economy. This perspective makes it necessary for contemporary scholars of labour, as well as those within the labour movement to acknowledge that the work structures within which labour finds itself are essentially social process[es] driven by human beings and human interests and not some phenomena imposed upon us" (SiD, 1997, p5). This recognition within social movement unionism in turn allows the assertion of the potential for human agency to challenge the status quo and change the situations that labour finds itself in, meaning human centred militancy is important to a vision appropriate to the era of globalisation" (Moody, 1997, p175).

Changes in the internal operation and makeup of the labour movement are also important if it intends to influence the global political economy in the future. This strand of social movement unionism highlights the importance of "social unionism within unions" (Waterman, 1999a, p5), a move away from "reliance on strict political structures, and towards a renewed rank and file democracy" (O'Brien, 2000b, p515). This signifies a shift back towards 'bottom- up' politics as opposed to the more 'top-down' politics that has dominated the labour movement in recent years (Williams, 1997). An optimistic perception of such changes sees them as allowing the labour movement to humanise, becoming open and transparent in operation, potentially increasing its popularity with workers who have expressed dissatisfaction with the closed door union politics of recent years (Waddington and Whitston, 1997).

By addressing the concerns and plights of workers and in

turn increasingly "act[ing] independently of political parties and address[ing] a wide range of social issues" (O'Brien, 2000b, p515), social movement unionism leads the labour movement towards a new position in contemporary socio-politics and global civil society. If successfully implemented, such a shift in organisation could result in better relations with members, society at large and potential members, providing the springboard towards the creation of a counter-hegemonic movement. There is the possibility however that those working within the labour movement may not be able to reconcile themselves with such humanising developments, as the practices and positions they have taken for granted will be threatened. Be it through a desire to maintain existing positions within hierarchies, or merely an unwillingness or incapacity to deal with change, it seems the human condition has the potential to limit the widespread redevelopment of the labour movement at all levels[3]. Yet such limitations, when encountered, seem to present a unique opportunity to completely renew itself, as 'old fashioned' elements are replaced with more forward thinking members and organisers.

The second key element of social movement unionism in the context of this research is its international focus (Waterman,

---

3. Interview with TUC Official, 27/6/2002.

1998, 1999b), designed to mirror the internationalisation of the state and capital (Cox, 1981). This internationalisation is of critical importance for the success of the labour movement, operating as it does in an era where "there can no longer be any effective trade union policy, even at a national level, that is not global in concept and international in organisation" (Gallin, 1994, p9). That social movement unionism shifts the labour movement towards being international in its scope is not necessarily new however.

In past decades it was true to say "the labour movement was international" (SiD, 1997, p5) due to co-operation between national union movements. But a recent period saw "trade unions and labour parties being more concerned with their national issues" (SiD, 1997, p5) in a bid to halt losses of power in an era which saw political and economic power being shifted towards the global and regional levels. In this sense labours' position within the global political economy appears to have stagnated, whilst those involved within capital structures, big business and governance have embraced the global agenda as a means of profiting and keeping power and influence. These latter elements of the global political economy may in turn actually be seen as having constructed the global agenda through policy and practice, rather than simply being passive victims of change, in the sense that some within the labour movement see themselves.

The co-operation, solidarity and action across borders that social movement unionism has at its heart, provides the labour movement with the potential to effect change within the current global order in a fashion that has been lacking in recent years (Dolvik, 1997, p5). This shift of operations up to supranational levels means the labour movement can match the global multilateralism (O'Brien et al eds. 2000) involving international organisations, nation states and capital that have supported the global hegemonic order. For if social movement unionism is being pursued, it is only by changing nationally based structures and processes, then transferring these onto the international stage that the labour movement can hope to influence political decisions taken within organisations such as the European Union (Hoffman and Hoffman, 2001).

Social movement unionism shows that a national centered myopia that sees the labour movement all too often "working within models developed under a national/industrial/colonial capitalism at a moment in which capitalism is becoming globalised" (Waterman, 1999a, p2) need not be accepted. Whilst the theoretical framework analysed in this chapter reinforces the important role that the nation state has to play in contemporary

IPE, bearing in mind the globalisation of production and the state, a "new global strategy for labour" (Munck, 1998, p2) is important if the labour movement is to challenge the supremacy of a capital system already geared towards action at the global level.

Again, we see here that social movement unionism is primarily based in a real world context, as there are already "intensive efforts to build labour solidarity across the emerging continental economy" (Rupert, 2000, p71) observable in areas such as the relatively politically developed Europe. Importantly however, whilst "unions have recognised the need to build global organising capacity" (Starr, 2000, p88), these moves are still in relative infancy and international institutions such as the ETUC still struggle to be taken seriously by political and economic bodies in the global political economy[4] Nonetheless, a sustained effort to develop social movement unionism at all levels including the global will go some way to providing what some have argued is only a natural form of resistance to global pressures (Stalker, 2000).

Such resistance is not afforded by divergent, loosely linked national labour movements that exist in the global political

---

4. Interview with ICFTU Official, 24I7/2002

economy, but rather by a labour movement able to mobilise and organise effectively both within and beyond the confines of nation states. It will be argued in this research that true internationalism will prove to be difficult however, as divergent practices, languages, traditions and priorities stand in the way of a unified global labour movement. There is also another potential pitfall for the globalising of the labour movement, for if the attempts to organise and co-operate are not matched by the satisfactory development of a form of institutional framework of structures (Turner, 1996, p325), confusion may rein. Whilst global organisations do currently exist in the guise of the ICFTU and WCL, their history has been fraught with conflict and their efficacy may be questioned[5]. Even the regional level that can be argued to represent a more manageable area of organisation and action than the global, sees an organisation such as the ETUC plagued by problems of diverging aims and goals[6] and a lack of legitimacy (Dolvik, 1997).

The third key element of social movement unionism is the

---

5. Interview with International Textile, Garment and Leather Workers Federation Official (IGTLWF), 7/8/2002

6. This insight comes from personal correspondence with Dr Peter Waterman, 29/2/2002.

call for the labour movement to "reach out to other social movements" (O'Brien, 2000b, p515) in order to reassert its position in the global political economy. This mirrors Gramscian claims that for effective moves towards counter-hegemony, a particular group must extend its focus beyond its own narrow interests to develop a coherent social bloc. In the current global political economy, there is a recognition that labour related issues can no longer be partitioned off from the rest of the global political economy (Munck, 1998), and instead all social issues are interrelated and reinforcing. Moves to promote discussion and organisation across civil society between divergent societal grouping provide a framework in which a social consensus against the current socio-political system (Rifkin, 1995) can be created. A central theme of social movement unionism and this research is that such increased "engagement with new social movements" (O'Brien, 2000b, p516) holds potential for the development of the labour movement as an effective body for social action.

By forging links to other movements, the labour movement will find itself in a position to learn new practices and skills from social movements (Munck, 1998) that in many cases were created in a much more contemporary period than labour bodies. This points towards a valuable process whereby ideas can in a sense be 'cross-pollinated' between social movements and the labour movement. Such a dynamic would allow labour to learn the new ways of "organising and operating" (Fairbrother, 2000, p59) integral to social movement unionism without being forced to completely disassemble itself. Yet in order that co-operation and linkages with other social movements are successful this research argues that the labour movement as a whole must address the issue of expanding its understanding of socio-politics. The framework for a successful strategy for social movement unionism will be analysed by looking to what extent issues other than those traditionally tied to the 'workplace', such as pay and protection, are being taken into account. Issues such as gender, race, the environment all are intertwined in the lives of workers represented by the labour movement, so to exclude such issues seems ill judged for organisations eager to gain influence.

Some examples of the labour movement successfully coordinating with other movements do exist, yet whilst these are growing in importance, they are still relatively rare. A key example of such co-operation was the 1996 cooperation between Childright (a children's rights organisation) and global unions that drew attention to the fact that a quarter of the 100,000 workers in the Pakistani football industry (producing footballs for western

Europe and beyond) were children under 15 (WCL, 2001, p4). This shows how successful a strategy of co-operation can be, yet problematically for potential moves to truly inclusive socio-politics, it is still firmly focused on the world of what the labour movement perceives to be 'work' and does not show a great broadening of the labour agenda. It is true that organised labour and social movements can work together towards certain common goals (Adkin, 1999, pp209-215), but it will require a change in focus on the part of the labour movement if it is to be a success. Indeed, given that today it is difficult to isolate workplace issues from those of wider society and vice versa[7], a change of policy from the labour movement is necessary if social movement unionism is to be fully implemented as a framework for redevelopment and repositioning of labour organisations.

There are some caveats to bear in mind regarding the implementation of social movement unionism as the contemporary conceptualisation for the future development of the labour movement. The first is to ensure that whilst within a social coalition where "broader social agendas" (Rupert, 2000, p84) are pursued, explicitly labour related issues are still given an important place on the agenda. For whilst it is true that in a

---

7. Interview with UNISON Official, 9/9/2002

pluralistic age of socio-politics, unions can not necessarily think of themselves as "the privileged representative of labour" (Waterman, 2000, p7), there seems little sense in them surrendering their position altogether.

If the labour movement is to retain its position as being more than simply another element of a general movement (Waterman and Wills, 2001) efforts will be necessary to ensure its strengths and experiences are retained. If this is successful the labour movement and the unions therein will not become simply another "NGO campaigning, lobbying and networking along with the rest of them" (Munck, 1998, p9), but will instead be at the forefront of the creation of a coherent counter-hegemonic bloc.

With this in mind, it is important that the strengths of the labour movement are not disregarded when arguing for a coalition model for the future. As even within a "broader coalition of social forces" (Cox, 2000, p29), labour has particular traditions and strengths that mean it is well placed to deal effectively with certain situations in the modern world. Due to its historical position near the centre of political frameworks and processes, labour is well versed in the intricacies of negotiating "agreements with governments or corporations" (O'Brien, 2000a, p45) that have in the past protected worker's positions. It also has in place both an "institutionalised structure and mechanisms for accountability" (O'Brien, 2000a, p45) that mean the members within are theoretically guaranteed to have their needs and wishes represented in a way that organisations with no accountability can't guarantee. Whilst reliance on these traditional, institutional forms of operating may be redundant in pursuit of a 'pure' social movement unionism, there are some discernible skills and practices that will prove important for a social coalition if it is to have success within the corridors of power.

When discussing social movement unionism and the calls for increased linkages to other social movements, a central question is how compatible the labour movement is with other social movements. As will be discussed in chapter three, it seems unlikely that the labour movement with its current institutionalised form and long standing traditions is entirely compatible with other more modern and dynamic groups. Indeed the current form of operating held by the labour movement can be argued to be the antithesis to the dynamism pointed towards by social movement unionism. This is a claim strongly refuted by figures within the labour movement, however, who claim that unions are not apart from society and social movements[8] and they

8. Interview with ETUC Official, 22/7/2002

are in fact much more 'true' social movements than others due to the inclusivity and democracy[9] inherent within the labour movement.

Despite such claims, it becomes apparent when the structures of the labour movement are analysed in this thesis, that "labour's tighter and more hierarchical organisation" (Cox, 1999, p19) is at odds with social movements' "far more loosely structured and more participatory forms of organisation" (Cox, 1999, p19). This leaves the question of whether the labour movement can work harmoniously with "social movements [that] are, by definition, fluid and large" (O'Brien et al eds. 2000, p15), and that evolve, transform and often lack a permanent institutional structure. There is "no central core" (O'Brien et al eds. 2000, p15) to many social movements, and that model is very different to labour's traditional, institutionalised structures, unable to match the fluidity and organic nature required by a 'new' social movement. Yet this research argues that such incompatibility merely highlights the key elements of change needed if the labour movement is to prosper. The traditional model is failing and the 'new' form of social movement appears to be more attuned to the socio-politics of the modern era, so a melding together of the two

9. Interview with ETUC Official, 22/7/2002

could be the way forward.

There are other theoretical points of concern regarding the conceptions behind social movement unionism. One such issue is the prefix of 'new' that is sometimes prefixed to the term social movement when discussed in relation to unions and the labour movement. When such a prefix is used we begin to encounter a "harsh juxtaposition between the (bad) old politics and the good (new) social movements" (Munck, 1998, p7) that can only be damaging and misleading. It must be recognised that the 'old' labour movement is still a valid form of social grouping, however. And, whilst it appears that much debate surrounding social movement unionism is pointing towards "the clash of old unionism and new social movements having a transformative effect on worker's organisations" (O'Brien, 2000a, p44), this thesis argues that the labour movement as it stands today is in need of redevelopment rather than complete rejection.

Interlinked to the problem of sign posting forms of organising as either 'new' or 'old' is the question of just how much of social movement unionism is actually new. It can be argued that much of what social movement unionism advocates is past practice of the labour movement (Walker, 1994). After all, the labour movement originated as a grass roots, militant movement, with an international focus due to its socialist beginnings (Waterman, 1998). And it is only in relatively recent years that the labour movement has found itself operating in a fashion ill-suited to deal effectively with the challenges posed by the world around it.

The final issue is that social movement unionism it may be seen as exclusive in nature because in academic discussions it primarily applies to organised elements of the labour movement, namely unions,. Unprotected workers, so prevalent in the modern global political economy, must be acknowledged in this research if it is to gain insights for more than only the most easily quantifiable and observable elements of labour (Phizacklea and Wolkowitz, 1995, pp1-19). Whilst there have been some attempts to bring unprotected labour into the IPE field of debate (Harrod, 1987; Amoore, 2002a), these appear to be exceptions to the norm. Because of this it is important that we move away from past IPE traditions where "the importance of organising informal sector workers is not equally recognised" (Gallin, 2001, p531), and instead recognise the importance of diverse and large groupings of workers who are in need of protection, particularly within the theoretical context provided by the Gramscian concepts of social relations and forces. In doing so the labour movement will be following an implication of social movement unionism that unions speak on behalf of a wider constituency than their membership alone.

Conclusion

It was argued above that Gramscian thought provides valuable conceptual tools to assist our understanding of the world today, as it allows for an understanding of the fashion in which societal forces and actors may challenge hegemony within the global political economy. This socially oriented approach to understanding IPE forms the bedrock of a theoretical approach underpinning this research, which also incorporates an understanding of the importance of excluded elements of society, and international dimensions to analysis. At the heart of this perspective is the belief that social agents have the power to operate together within civil society to co-ordinate and develop a unified resistance to the pressures of globalisation.

Social movement unionism, a model for action that relies implicitly on Gramscian and neo-Gramscian concepts of hegemony, social relations and forces, and counter-hegemony, has been shown to be an important framework for the future of the labour movement. This is due to the changes proposed for the movement's current formations and practices, with the related adoption of more dynamic and militant approaches being observable across the globe. With its core themes of internationalisation, changes in attitude and moves towards social coalitions, it is argued in this research that trade unions will only truly be viable in the future if they adopt this model of organising and action, with social movements being used as a template for trade union development.

Social movements, the inspiration for social movement unionism, were argued in this chapter to be difficult to identify or quantify. But this research rests upon an understanding that they are fluid, mobile and dynamic forms of social association. They also have most commonly, but not exclusively, a goal of influencing or impacting upon particular facets of the global political economy. Building on this understanding of the foundations of social movement unionism, this thesis will analyse how social movement unionism is being implemented in contemporary labour politics, and the extent to which its central themes are being used by trade unions keen to reposition themselves in a global political economy riddled with challenges for workers and their representatives.

By carrying through a central, explicit acknowledgement of Gramscian concepts and their neo-Gramscian utilisation, this research will constantly seek to understand the tensions at play within the labour movement, and how they may hamper an effective revival of the movement as a social agent. In this sense it is argued that Gramscian concepts may help to bring about an understanding of modern IPE that has the potential for human agency at its core, especially if differing human experiences are brought together, as a social movement unionism that challenges prevailing attitudes and norms is built. The next chapter will continue to place the arguments of this research in context, by analysing the challenges and opportunities presented to the labour movement by the processes of globalisation.

2. GLOBALISATION AND LABOUR: CHALLENGES AND OPPORTUNITIES

Introduction

G lobalisation is a common explanatory idea in social science, and at times it resembles a panacea as a dominant explanatory tool in much of IPE literature. Its use can at times appear somewhat vague and excessive (Barry Jones, 1995), due to the concept's complex nature that defies simple classification or blanket usage. A rigorous understanding of globalisation acknowledges that the term represents "not a single, unified phenomenon, but a syndrome of processes and activities" (Mittelman, 2000, p4), that present both severe challenges and key opportunities to many different elements of the global political economy, including the labour movement.

This chapter will present analysis of globalisation's key elements, with specific attention being paid to their consequences for the modern labour movement, in order to understand the contemporary context in which workers and labour organisations find themselves. For despite assertions that globalisation is still more a myth than a reality (Hirst, 1997; Douglas, 2000), there is an observable interlinked set of processes and interactions

(Gamble and Payne, 1996) with important implications for labour.

Theorists differ as to which are the central forces of globalisation, with some arguing that "technological change, consumerism, and neo-liberal economic policies" (Stillwell, 2000, p3) are critical, whilst others contend that "more frequent access with foreign cultures" (Hodson, 1997, p5) is key. This research begins with the notion that globalisation is an intricate web of processes borne out of and developed by neo-liberal policies and practices, that has enabled capital to "pursue its market logic with a relentlessness that has not been evident since the first decades of the industrial revolution" (Falk, 2000, p67). Yet, despite being equated with a modern, capital-led era, it is not valid to equate globalisation solely with a capital led "exploitation of labour" (Stillwell, 2000, pl). Instead this chapter will highlight certain positive dimensions that are presented to workers through the processes of globalisation of production; technology; governance and civil society.

By focusing on the implications of globalisation for labour, this chapter goes against a trend in IPE where "the financial system has taken centre stage" (O'Brien, 1999, p2) as the "state-firm universe" (O'Brien, 1999, p2) has occupied academic attention. Such a focus has reflected a world in which "the economic aspect is primary: it is the multilateral gains that can be achieved from open access to markets that make globalisation attractive" (Hodson, 1997, p5). Yet there are some within the global political economy that recognise the importance of workers. In recent years we have seen the Secretary General of the UN Kofi Annan argue that "workers play such a key role in wealth creation" (UN 2000a) that to neglect their needs is no longer acceptable.

From this argument stems an assertion that "labour is not a commodity" (ILO, 2000e, p3), and must instead be understood as a social force critical in all aspects of modern society. The acknowledgement of the importance of workers around the world provides impetus for analysts and theorists including ILO Director General Juan Somavia "to put a human face on the global political economy...[and to] recognise we need to affect the future of social development" (Somavia, 1999a, pp 1-2). Yet to simply present a human face to globalisation could be interpreted as a shift to mask the exploitative dynamics at work in the global age, instead it is incumbent upon the labour movement in particular to strive for a societal response to such dynamics. In doing so it is possible that a current situation where "economic inequalities grow, between those able to avail themselves of the opportunities opened up by the globalisation of capital and those who bear its social costs" (Stillwell, 2000, p2) be effectively challenged by social actors.

The first process of globalisation to be discussed is the globalisation of production, a term signifying the development of transnational structures, procedures and relations that form the productive dimension of political economy (Cox, 1987). The importance of any shifts towards globalisation within the production structure is of great consequence for labour, as changes in employment, forms of work and structures within which labour operates, impact on socio-political practices and structures that surround it.

The Globalisation of Production

The Gramscian-inspired theoretical framework that this research rests upon holds the position of production as central to the whole of the political economy, as it is the structure that provides "not only...the supply of the physical requisites of life but also...the creation of the institutions and relationships through which life goes on and through which the accumulation of resources that sustain power and authority takes place" (Cox,

1987, p396). In more succinct terms, the social relations that are embodied within the organisations, practices and structures of production impact upon all of "social life" (Cox, 1987, p 1).

As was shown in the analysis of Gramscian inspired thought in the previous chapter, the production structure and social relations therein are intertwined with the forms of state and world orders that exist at any one time within the global political economy. Because of this relationship, "changes in the organisation of production generate new social forces which, in turn, bring about changes in the structure of states; and the generalisation of changes in the state alters the problematic of world order" (Cox, 1981, p138). This essentially means that changes in production have implications for all other aspects of socio-political life. This conceptualisation has been given credence in recent years as analysis of the post- World War II era highlighted how American forms of production were consolidated at home, then exported abroad, meaning that in time a hegemonic order was developed with the US the dominant force (Rupert, 1995).

The contemporary era has seen similarly significant changes in production that has implications for the political economy, namely an increasing shift towards "global organisations of production" (Cox, 1993, p259) that has been a central element of the wider processes of globalisation. This shift has had associated consequences that would be expected from Gramscian-inspired thought, including the "internationalisation of the state.[and] the restructuring of national societies and the emergence of a global structure" (Cox, 1993, pp260-261). This following section will analyse the processes, structures and agents within this globalisation of production, and will show the consequences for the labour movement.

Central to the globalising of production that has included changes in the geographical positioning, social composition and practical performance of work has been the growth in importance of the Multi-National Corporation (MNC). Through an increasing ability to transcend national borders and labour markets by shifting their production sites to different areas of the world (Dicken, 1998), these MNCs have been agents of globalisation. This is due to the fashion by which they have transferred particular practices and structures across the globe, contributing to the creation and maintenance of a dominant world order. Truly multinational operations increased in recent decades, with "the establishment of manufacturing facilities abroad" (Dicken, 1992, p52) being a prevalent practice amongst companies in a position to do so. The furniture company IKEA was an extreme example of shifts towards global production, and subcontracting, a "subcontracts all the actual manufacture of goods it sells, using about 2300 firms of various size located in seventy countries" (Hoogvelt, 2001, p 105).

For capital, such shifts in organisation and practice appear clear, as relocation, subcontracting and fragmentation allow for the minimising of costs and risks for the Host Company. But the situation facing affected labour is somewhat different, with increased job insecurity permeating all areas of the global production structure, with the perception that jobs are in constant threat from imminent relocation. This globalising tendency has moved beyond traditional manufacturing in recent years, and has moved to incorporate many other sectors such as semi-service call centre work, or data input service. Essentially we now see a picture in which all elements of work can be relocated, meaning that in turn, all workers are affected by global change.

Despite initial appearances however, the real map of globalised production is perhaps not entirely global, for there exists an "enormous geographical unevenness" (Dicken, 1998, p26) amongst differing areas of the globe that export or import work. The fragmentation of production undertaken by capital means that often production is still "concentrated in a relatively small number of countries" (Dicken, 1998, p27), and the true situation is often argued to be one of international regionalisation rather than globalisation. Certain areas of the world such as Europe and America retain key elements of the production structure including research and development that are often skills intensive or prestigious, whilst less developed areas are responsible for production, with the least developed areas being totally excluded from the economic map (Cox, 1987. p245). That the operations exported from the developed core often end up in developing areas of the globe highlights problems for workers, as work is relocated to areas outside the traditional 'strong' western labour movement's protective reach that focuses on the developed world.

Indeed less developed nations may make concessions regarding labour standards within their borders in order to secure investment, and companies in search of profits are often eager to accept regardless of the human impact of low wages and lack of social protection. Workers find themselves operating within an environment where social safety nets such as union protection or legislation protecting workers that may be perceived as contrary to free market principles held by MNCs are abolished thus leaving workers with no real choice in what employment they take, or voice to demand and protect acceptable wages or standards. Such a situation is not confined to developing countries however, anti-trade union legislation in Britain during the 1980s and 90s can be argued to represent a tool to open up the economy to foreign investment.

The labour movement as a whole is therefore faced by a situation whereby as a particular state or region gains investment through lower regulation and cheap labour, other countries can follow suit, thus "setting off a downward spiral of deteriorated labour standards" (SiD, 1997, p3). As such, to a certain extent the growth in "labour market deregulation can be seen as a consequence of MNC influence, either directly through political processes or indirectly through decisions to restrict investment to particular countries" (Hodson, 1997, p22). These implications of the globalisation of production present the labour movement with the need to co-ordinate action across spatial boundaries to counteract pressures that pay little heed to national borders. In doing so there can be a reaction to a situation where "the world has become not only one global market- but one global labour market" (SiD, 1997, p3) with workers most often being cast as the victim.

Within this globalisation of production, low wage labour is not necessarily the only concern for capital when locating operations, although it is often of prime importance (Van Der Knaap and Le Heron, 1995). Other concerns such as developed transportation networks; the availability of raw materials; labour flexibility; and the availability of well-educated workers can all affect decisions to relocate production, particularly to areas that have become industrial clusters such as areas within India or the Far East, where efforts have been made to provide suitable sites for investment (Dicken, 1998). This means that it is problematic to equate the globalisation of production simply as a process of deteriorating standards from workers, as instead there are other elements internal to what is a complex process. Despite this, low wages and poor labour protection are both issues that the labour movement can identify and attempt to visibly counteract, and for this reason they are often of prime concern for those within trade unions at all levels.

Despite the undeniable pressures of globalisation, analysis of spatial shifts in production must be cautious. It has been forcibly argued that much concern stems not from concrete reality, but rather a case of perception. Indeed it is arguable that for many MNCs "the global corporation is still more myth than reality, [but] it is one which now exercises a powerful hold over the strategic vision as well as the management styles of large corporations with international connections and markets" (Axford, 1995, p98). In such a situation we see not simply footloose corporations and capital, but rather a large proportion of companies with ties "to particular countries remain[ing] strong" (Axford, 1995, p97), with often the mere perception that companies have a global reach presenting them with power over other socio-political actors.

As with all issues in IPE, this argument is a contentious one, with contrary positions stating that on the one hand "there are almost no really big businesses that are not transnational" (Strange, 1988, p74), and on the other "of the largest 100 firms in the world, not one is truly 'global', 'footloose' or 'borderless'" (Ruigrok and Van Tulder, 1995, p159). Yet what must be acknowledged is that the ability, either real or perceived, of companies to shift production around the globe holds great consequences for labour.

Even if companies are not "placeless corporations" (Mittelman, 1997, p 11) when strict criteria are applied, the perceptions held by those outside often differ. The fear held by political and social leaders that a company may shift its operations from one area to another means that governments and other host groups are eager to provide acceptable contexts for investors, even if a result of this is lowering standards for labour as discussed above. This has led to a situation whereby for years MNCs have played "off national states against one another" (Beck, 2000, p65) to gain the best circumstances for their relocation, meaning that states, afraid of losing investment will do more to attract and then keep their MNC 'guests' happy, be it through market deregulation or financial inducement.

In situations where the mobility of capital becomes reality, and production is shifted from one area of the globe to another, the consequences are often devastating. Economic and social ruin is often left behind in the area vacated as sudden unemployment, and the resulting social and economic problems, hit a particular area at a precise moment. It is often to avoid such damaging circumstances that states may abandon past practices such as those that provide protection for labour, as well as offering financial incentives and subsidies in the hope of securing financial gain (Thomas, 1997). Yet these strategies designed to entice and keep investment have the potential to impact on workers in just as negative a fashion as the loss of production from an area would have, as workers can find themselves without protection, representation or suitable incomes. States pursuing policies which place workers in such situations may be seen not as taking command of their own situation, but rather playing little more than a courtesan role to capital, "beholden to more powerful interests in the global political economy, submissive m its policies ...as choices are restrained" (Mittelman, 2000, p26).

Despite the very real challenges facing the labour movement that result from these developments, there are opportunities presented to the labour movement. As traditional state borders become more permeable in today's world, some workers have the potential to move around an ever-growing market place in search of employment (Stalker, 2000) in a similar fashion to mobile capital. Most often the elements of labour most able to shift are perhaps the most affluent, in less need of a new situation, with experienced and sought after specialised workers being mobile, whilst many more poor workers still unable to match capital's mobility. Crucially then, much of this mobility is mere potential as many workers are still unable to fund expensive wholesale moves. For those unable to afford the move, illegal immigration is an option as unscrupulous elements seek profits from low skilled workers around the globe (Van Der Knaap and Le Heron, 1995) an act that often places such workers in the unprotected and overlooked informal economy.

In developing a coordinated challenge to the current status quo through social alliance and maneuvering, the labour movement faces the interests and influences of the "transnational capitalist class" (Sklair, 1991, p53), in a sense replicating the traditional concept of class conflict in the global age. This cadre consists of "top owners and key executives of transnationals, central and other international bankers ...leading politicians and civil servants" (Gill, 1990, p94) whose interests are served through the promotion and protection of the neo-liberal economic and political world order.

If we are to believe the arguments that this transnational class is growing stronger and becoming increasingly united (Sklair, 1991) then the labour movement will not go unchallenged as it attempts to shape the world around it. But without a coherent pursuit of societal change by the labour movement, we could witness a period where MNCs, increasingly mobile in their operations and complimented by this transnational, coherent and organised social grouping, are left free to dictate the trajectory of the global political economy's development. Such a situation would simply serve to push labour further onto the defensive, so it is necessary that the "genuinely transnational trade unions" (Sklair, 1991, p64) that exist are developed into the central core of an increasingly co-ordinated and dynamic labour movement spanning all levels of action.

The globalisation of production discussed here has not occurred simply through the will power of capital however. Instead it has been facilitated through the development and implementation of new forms of technology that have provided easier transportation, communication and indeed performance of work. For this reason it is "a fallacy to consider production in isolation from research and technology" (Howells and Wood, 1993, p7), and the globalisation of technology and the impacts that has had on workers and the work they perform will now be discussed.

The Globalisation of Technology

The globalisation of production has only been enabled through technological advances such as those in communications, transport and mechanisation whose "destabilising ...effects are being felt all over the world" (Rifkin, 1995, p198). And whilst such a recognition of the importance of technology is necessary, it is important we do not fall foul of 'technological determinism'. For in discussing the new information age where "technologies [have] played a decisive role in facilitating" (Castells, 2000, p368) change, we must remember that technology "does not cause particular kinds of change" (Dicken, 1998, p145), instead it is a product of societal development and a tool created as the needs and wishes of society develop.

Technology does not exist within a void, and it is "the needs of the economy dictate that new technological methods must be implanted" (Kagarlitsky, 1999, p83) rather than the reverse. And alarmingly for workers within the global political economy, it can appear that "with every turn in the spiral of technological revolution, more and more new contradictions and disproportions accumulate" (Kagarlitsky, 1999, p3).

Electronic communications technology has been central to the processes of globalisation that are affecting the lives of workers today. Whereas half a century ago communication across distance was difficult, the contemporary reality is different, with the Internet, mobile phone and traditional communications technology revolutionising the way certain areas of the globe operate (Mohammadi et al eds. 1997). In a sense "technological progress has compressed the time-space equation enormously" (Harvey, 1989, p125), meaning that contact can be made with the other side of the globe through the click of a button. It is this shrinkage of geographical limits that may be seen as having been a driving force behind the globalisation of production, as a company may now have several different bases spread across the globe, communicating quickly and efficiently in order that normal running is maintained. Simultaneously, changes in transport technology such as faster, more efficient air travel, have allowed for the quicker transport of goods and products around the world, meaning that production sites can be far removed from target markets or destinations.

Just as technology has allowed for production to be shifted in this fashion, it has also brought substantial changes to the very nature of work, often through assisting and replacing human agency. In the 'Post-Fordist workplace', many industrial sectors have long seen "intelligent machinery...replac[e] human beings in countless tasks" (Rifkin, 1995, p3). For capital this mechanisation makes sense, as after an initial investment there are no union worries, no contract negotiations, and no 'human problems' such as sickness or stress. Instead when the computers and machines know what to do, they do it (Milkman, 1997). The increasing prevalence of machinery in the workplace has served to place labour on the defensive in the face of unemployment and job insecurity. The more traditional manufacturing industries of the U.S. present a good example of these processes, where "between 1981 and 1991, more than 1.8 million manufacturing jobs disappeared" (Rifkin, 1995, p8) as companies turned to technology in the search for efficiency and profits.

Quite plainly, this strand of technological development leads to increased job insecurity for workers operating where technology can potentially do the same job either more efficiently or cheaper. Yet even if jobs remain in place, workers can also be threatened as increases in the use of technology mean that skills needed to perform tasks are changing (Hodson, 1997), rendering some workers unable to compete. The sectors and companies most affected by these technological developments are often areas in which manual, male labour has predominated, in other words former strongholds of unions. This means that when jobs are lost so are trade union members, a process that has weakened the labour movement, in turn leading to a vicious cycle whereby weakened unions are unable to adequately protect and represent remaining members.

The influences of technology are not confined to manufacturing, however, and many workers find themselves in new forms of employment that are often made possible by the globalisation of technology, such as call centres. In such forms of areas, work is often highly stressful, poorly paid, and has draconian aspects to them, such as highly scrutinised working procedures, minimal breaks, and difficult and unreliable hours. This is in no small part due to the absence of union participation, as these industries are often the result of governmental efforts to gain investment through sidelining the labour movement, or unions are simply too weak to attempt successful strategies for gaining a foothold[10].

As well as replacing traditional jobs with mechanisation, or shifting work to new sectors, technology has also facilitated a shift of work away from a traditional workplace. Today many workers can be seen to work from home, often performing menial duties for companies eager to cut costs. In this sense telephones and computers and other forms of technology have facilitated a wholesale change in what is meant by the term work, as we can no longer rely on outdated concepts of what work done where and by whom. The result of this shift away from the

---

10. Interview with GMB Official. 27/5/2002.

traditional workplace is again a rise in unprotected, unrepresented workers, as traditional labour organisations are either ill-equipped or ill-prepared to attempt to incorporate these workers into their remit and address the issues that they face. The central theme of social movement unionism that informs this research, shows it is important for the labour movement to acknowledge this challenge, and through a widening of union focus, address the issues of large numbers of workers in need of assistance who are currently outside their remit.

Integral to such shifts in the way work is performed are shifts away from traditional, full time employment towards more "contingent workforces in order to respond quickly to market fluctuations" (Rifkin, 1995, p204). Rather than having traditional full-time workforces, the changes detailed here mean that many companies can either not afford the ongoing financial demand of having full time, permanent staff, or do not need them. Due to this we see increases in the "use of flexible labour with short-term contracts or contracts with an unspecified duration, leaving the employer free to decide when to dismiss a worker" (Ruigrok and Van Tulder, 1995, p45), in order that flexibility is at a maximum and costs are kept low. Simultaneously, we can observe a widespread trend towards increases in part time employment that lacks many of the benefits of full time employment such as security, higher wages and guaranteed hours (Fernandez Kelly, 1989).

In terms of the increases in part-time and casual employment at least, we see women being most affected. Indeed the term 'feminisation of work' seen in IPE can be taken to represent not only a growing number of active female workers but also a trend towards "the flexibilisation and casualisation of labour" (Marchand and Runyan, 2000, p 17), through increases in "part time, temporary or contracted unprotected workers" (Amoore, 2002a, p142).

Indeed, whilst part time work accounts for a quarter of all employment, it already represents approximately half of all female employment, highlighting the disproportionate amount of women in precarious positions in the global economy (Walters, 2002). This growth in part time work is not geographically concentrated either (Ruberry et al, 1998, p34), and instead we can observe, "in all countries the majority of part-time workers are women" (Bullock, 1994, p21). This is an extreme example of how changes within the production structure can affect huge swathes of people's lives as changes in social relations lead here to "new forms of work, multiple strategies of social protection, different lifestyles ...are unsettling and reshaping women's lives" (Wichterich, 2000, pvii).

The sectors of work within which women and other marginalised groups find themselves are "often the least organised" (Bullock, 1994, p132) by the labour movement. Indeed, it is also argued that when unions are present in workplaces with men and other groups including women, there are examples of unions standing by and watching as women lose jobs or are placed in a more perilous position because "the male workforce is being protected at the expense of the female" (Bullock, 1994, p24). This highlights the fashion in which informal and non-traditional workers operating in the modern global political economy "can rarely look towards unions for improving their bargaining power" (Rowbotham and Mitter, 1994, p20).

When pressed on the issue of bringing such non-standard workers, particularly women, into the labour movement's focus, a Transport and General Worker's Union (TGWU) figure in Britain argued that a central element of their plans was a 'change of image'[11] rather than a change of content, an example of which is a change of union logo as discussed in the next chapter. There are some who understand more explicitly the labour movement's need for women members if their membership is to prosper (Grint, 1998,

---

11. Interview with TGWU Official, 9/9/2002

p216), but there are simultaneous perspectives that argue to look beyond traditional constituencies may "suggest the exhaustion of the traditional trade union movement" (Waterman, 2001, p185), something that some may rather choose to deny than address. Indeed the pursuit of "new directions and instruments" (Wichterich, 2000, p33) for the future is often rejected by those in the labour movement as is shown throughout this book.

The processes of globalising production and changes in technology that have served to challenge workers, also present the labour movement with certain opportunities in its move to respond to globalisation. Specifically, "developments in mass communications" (Gill, 1993, p 15) can form a central element of labour's attempts to organise and mobilise its constituent parts around the globe. For whilst the processes of globalisation have propagated a technological age where capital is mobile around the world, there is the potential for workers and labour organisations to use the same technologies to co-operate and co-ordinate across boundaries.

The labour movement can use this ability to transfer information across national borders, and co-ordinate itself in simultaneous demonstrations and protests around the world through communications media (Moody, 1997). In this sense technology is a tool that allows more efficient action on behalf of workers as new forms of protest such as electronic mail posting or petitioning allows widespread action. Technology can also be used to break down barriers to inclusion facing some workers, as those fortunate enough to have technological access may join unions and become part of their strategies without the need to be at a physical place. Union websites that provide information on worker's rights, how to join a union and contact links are a good example of such moves in the contemporary labour movement environment.

The globalisation of technology and production discussed here do not take place within a vacuum however, and instead the political and social frameworks that contextualise developments must be understood. Just as the production structure and technology have globalised, so to a degree have the frameworks of governance in the modern global political economy. Again, just as was the case with production, the picture may not be one of even globalisation, but regional groupings such as the EU present examples of an increasing globalisation of governance that mirrors the dimensions of capital. The following section will move to discuss this global dimension of governance in the modern world.

The Globalisation of Governance

To some it appears that the state is waning (Bauman, 1998; Strange, 1996) in the face of an "economy-capital [that] moves fast enough to keep permanently a step ahead of any (territorial, as ever) polity which may try to contain and redirect its travels" (Bauman, 1998, p55). Indeed it may be argued "while the world has become much more highly integrated economically, the mechanisms for managing the system in a stable, sustainable way have lagged behind" (Commission on Global Governance, 1995, pp135-136).

Yet even with the nation state being challenged "from above by the tugs of ...globalisation" (Mittelman, 2000, p26), it is hasty to write it off and in turn write off a key site of contestation for the labour movement. More plausible than the assertion that the state is withering away, is that the functions the nation state performs are changing and a form of "internationalisation of the state" (Cox, 1993, p260) is occurring.

Because of changes within the social relations of production, the system of governance is being affected through a need to similarly globalise. With capital operating above national borders, "states are no longer expected to perform most of the functions once seen as the raison d'etre of the nation state bureaucracies" (Bauman, 1998, p59), and instead we see international and global organisations take over certain responsibilities to allay arguments surrounding globalisation that imply the world economy is out of control (Hirst, 1997).

With the globalisation of production having "shifted the pack of cards and dealt them out differently both to states as players and to social groups as players" (Strange, 1988, p79), the ability of particular states to control their own destiny and that of others is not as strong as once thought. For some this implies that nation states are becoming individual 'competitive states', competing for prosperity and investment, and in some examples survival, in a similar vein to companies (Porter, 1990, p19). Yet whilst it has already been argued above that states are keen to secure investment and prosperity via various means (Dicken, 1998, p86), to equate globalisation simply with such a radical transformation of the nation state is somewhat hasty.

Governance is not simply the search for profits in the same way as a corporation acts. The provision of goods and services for inhabitants are still primary goals, and are obligations that companies do not have. As such the nation state is the guardian of its inhabitants, comprising governmental institutions and practices that provide the frameworks of national socio-political life. With this in mind one can understand the growing importance of the internationalising of the state via an increasing importance of international organisations of governance.

Following a Gramscian-inspired theoretical framework it is however, possible to understand how changes in production have led to similar changes in governance. With social relations shifting towards a more globalised, and in a sense fractured formation due to globalised production, the geographically constrained form of state has become complemented by forms of organisation more suited to dealing with global pressures. Bodies such as the European Union (EU) allow for a certain re-articulation of control, power and agency m the contemporary political system through co-operation and consultation (O'Brien et al eds. 2000) across borders. This process shifts governance to the level at which modern capital operates, and is as much an economic and political response as it is a societal response to globalising pressures.

Even with the proliferation of international bodies, individual nation states still have a pivotal role to play, as it is at this level that social and political consensus is formed and struggle takes place. Essentially the internationalisation of the state is only facilitated through the agreement of national bodies, and the pooling of their sovereignty that allows the creation and legitimisation of such bodies. In turn it is national frameworks for organisation and action that allow and initiatives or policies from the global and regional levels to be implemented (Terry and Towers, 2000, p1). In such a global system where power is effectively shifted upwards, states can be seen to act as agents of representation (Featherstone, 1993), the global electors who ensure that international organisations are answerable to people (Hirst, 1997). Essentially the nation state is still pivotal, at the very least as being a middleman between the populous and higher organisations, a source of legitimacy and a means of implementing the decisions of the supranational bodies within state borders.

Yet the growth of supranational bodies reflects the inequality often engendered by globalisation as often it is the most important states that find themselves benefiting from developments (Hirst, 1997). Instead less successful or important states often almost 'hang on the coat tails' of key countries, joining secondary organisations in attempts to secure their positions within the global hierarchy. This fracturing of the political system is already occurring with the G3 group of 'super-states' playing the primary role of overseer in global political discussions, much as a single hegemonic state would do in other world orders. That there has been a process of internationalising for the state in recent years is important for the current world order, as it ensures that globalised capital does not operate in a lawless system. This in turn means that workers and their organisations have a framework within which they can attempt to effect change through political and social action.

The European regional arena can in a sense be seen as the most important test arena for the globalisation of governance, presenting as it does an arena in which states form the nexus of a body mediating both "hyper liberalism and state capitalism" (Cox, 1993, p272). The success of such a co-operative arena would further cement the future of the nation state an integral piece of the global political arena, as the provision of a social, economic and political area based upon interstate co-operation and co-ordination would mean that pessimistic views regarding the end of the state's usefulness are ill-judged.

Within such an international governmental formation, the labour movement finds itself still operating with defined structures and not fluid dimensions. This is critical for an effective response to globalisation but means that the labour movement must be able to similarly shift its operations upwards in order that it operates on a level akin to that of capital and governance. Whilst in the past it has been argued that attempts on behalf of labour to organise above the national level were in vain (Strange, 1988, 1996), there do exist at present a series of international organisations that could, if developed effectively, succeed to address the issues of workers above the national level. These include at the global level the International Labour Organisation (ILO), World Confederation of Labour (WCL) and International Confederation of Free Trade Unions (ICFTU), and at the important European level the European Trade Union Confederation (ETUC) that co-ordinates with regional and national bodies to promote labour's interests.

Regardless of the extent of such organisation's successes to date, they do bring international attention to the issues important for workers, by apparently moving beyond national confines and calling for capital to "respect social fundamentals" (WCL, 1999a, p1) and "improve the conditions and the quality of life of people" (Somavia, 1999a, p2) across the globe.

Within a system such as this where politics is operating at the global and regional levels, it is plausible that we may observe a form of civil society emerge at an international level as a counterpart to globalised political society. Such a formation would represent a battleground where labour could gain a true voice as the "failure to build a social dimension to globalisation" (TUAC, 1997, p4). With the nation state still remaining an important political body, and with political power and influence in many instances shifting upwards, there are "networks that extend across levels of analysis and state borders" (Lipschutz, 1992. p390) that can be observed in the modern global political economy. Indeed following a Gramscian perspective that sees the state as culmination of political and civil society, it is arguable that an emerging form of global civil society inevitably complements the globalised political society. This research now outlines the debate surrounding the globalisation of civil society, as it is a necessary foundation for the internationalisation of the labour movement.

The Globalisation of Civil Society

Gramscian civil society is seen as "a contested space, established and extended by collective action, and composed of voluntary associations distinct from economy and, while not completely separate from, nonetheless outside the direct control of the state" (Mittelman, 1997, p30). In this conception civil society is the societal counterpart to the political society, a separate battleground where elements and organisations of society (e.g.

Non-Governmental Organisations (NGOs) and Trade Unions) interact and bid to gain support and join with others, potentially with the view to creating a viable alternative vision of the future in the form of a counter-hegemonic bloc.

Stemming from Gramscian studies of the national level of socio-politics, civil society has in the past been by definition national (Shaw, 1997). Yet the growing globalisation of governance as discussed above would presuppose the emergence of a civil society to accompany political society within a wider, globalised political formation. As changes in governance increasingly reflect the way that traditional forms of "thinking, acting and living within state-cum-social spaces and identities collapses in the course or economic, political, ecological, cultural and biographical globalisation" (Beck, 2000, p65), it can in tum be argued that there is an emergent form of global civil society.

As with social movements, there are numerous arguments surrounding global civil society. Again, this concept cannot be pinned down by the use of simplistic definitions, but some characteristics are highlighted within debate. First is the idea that Global Civil Society (GCS) is a sphere of action inherently "distinct from the architecture of states and markets" (Amoore and Langley, 2004, p89). This allows GCS to be seen as a true area of societal contestation, within which social agents including workers may work towards building a position of strength in a bid to effect change on the world around them. It is important however, that one recognises that civil society is not abstracted from the political or economic spheres. Instead it exists within a complicated intertwined network. And it is within this global civil society that consent has been developed in the past for a hegemonic world order in the post war period, built upon social relations of production and the related issues of political and economic formation (Rupert, 1993, p88).

The second defining concept of contemporary global civil society is that it comprises not coercive structures, but rather "networks, new social movements, NGOs, and other informal citizens groups" (Pasha and Blaney, 1998, p425). This can lead to an assumption that in this global age where many pressures affecting divergent people are the same, there is some commonality and coherence at the core of civil society. But it must be remembered that a "politics of connection is not necessarily a politics of a united front or a counter-hegemonic strategy" (Walker, 1994, p699), so to observe societal groupings at an international level should not lead to an assumption of a coordinated movement within a civil society. This is due to differing agendas; priorities;

and actions that may render divisions between social groups within global civil society.

Many IPE theorists have contributed to a growing discourse surrounding this conflictual GCS. These include amongst others Robert Cox (1983, 1999), Martin Shaw (1998), Robert Walker (1994), Stephen Gill (1991), Ronnie Lipschutz (1992), and Louise Amoore and Paul Langley (2004) but there is not necessarily a fundamental agreement as to the fundamental aspects of GCS between these works and this research.

Lipschutz pursues an avenue of analysis that argues GCS is a space autonomous "from the constructed boundaries of the state system" (Lipschutz, 1992, p391). Yet such a definition can lead to an oversight of the integral part that civil society plays in the makeup of the state, and by extension the global level of governance. This conception of GCS sees it as emerging due to certain key processes, namely the replacement of anarchy within states by a form of "norm-governed global system rooted in the global capitalist consumer culture" (Lipschutz, 1992, p390), the growing "inability of states to deal with certain ...problems" (Lipschutz, 1992, p390), and the "growth of new forms of political and social identity" (Lipschutz, 1992, p390).

It is vital that in pursuing such a conception one does not

over-emphasise a rejection or breakdown of the state system, as the nation state as an important and effective element in the contemporary system of governance. As was discussed in previous sections, even in the global age the nation state still has a particularly critical role to play. In turn this research acknowledges the fact that GCS is intrinsically linked to a shifting of power and action, but does not go so far as to argue that those following the "code of civil society" (Lipschutz, 1992, pp396) are denying the primacy or sovereign rights of states.

Instead this research argues that GCS operates alongside the traditional national level, within a complex web of interdependence within which global, regional and national levels interact with and reinforce each other. Those operating at the global level of civil society must be prepared and able to "interact with states" (Lipschutz, 1992, p396) in an effective manner, and not just merely project their efforts on the global stage. But such a recognition of the nation state does not lead naturally to an argument that "claims about an emerging global civil society ...usually reveal the productive powers of statist discourse more than they do the capacity of social movements to challenge that discourse" (Walker, 1994, p674). Rather it presents a balanced foundation upon which the transformative powers of GCS may rest. This places GCS as a major site of contestation that "allows for the construction of new political spaces" (Lipschutz, 1992, 391), "necessarily intertwined and mutually constituting" (Amoore and Langley, 2004, p93) a trinity between itself, economy and state.

Building on this is the explicit understanding of GCS as a "grassroots but transnational challenge to the realist idea of a nation-state system" (Pasha and Blaney, 1998, p425) comprising networks and associations operating within a space distinct from the direct control of, but inextricably linked to the state system. Here the challenges and opportunities presented by the processes of globalisation to political and social norms may "open up new potential for counter-hegemonic and progressive forces to begin to make transnational links, and thereby to insert themselves in a more differentiated, multilateral order" (Gill, 1991a, p311). Such an understanding presents this research with a basis to acknowledge the transformative arena in which the labour movement finds itself, and the central position this GCS has in the modern global political economy, whilst not rejecting links to the political-economic frameworks.

Cox, who argues that GCS may be seen as a "surrogate for a revolution that seems unlikely to happen" (Cox, 1999, p4) takes this further. Looking at a world in which the processes of globalisation have broken the once theoretically homogenous working class that was seen as the vehicle for revolution, into sub-factions each more or less integrated into globalised production, it is possible to observe how new forms of action are critical. Frameworks and social relations that have stretched across national borders give "a new material basis of civil society" (Cox, 1999, p10) that is not just a collection of actors, but rather is a dynamic "realm of contesting ideas" (Cox, 1999, p10) within which divisions must be dealt with if the peoples of the world are to build a counter-hegemonic project.

Due to the fracturing of once strong class formations, and the alienation of many societal groups from the traditional political system, action within this GCS will at least initially be focused on co-operation, alliance building and "collective self-help" (Cox, 1993). These processes could in time lead to the creation of a grouping strong enough to present a counter-hegemonic vision to the prevailing world order. In this sense we see an opportunity for the labour movement to use GCS to begin the long process of building social alliances and coalitions, central elements of social movement unionism, as the labour movement can reach out to other movements in order to learn new skills and develop societal partnerships suited to the modern age.

But despite arguments that the labour movement is somehow a rightful leader of civil society at all levels, with "trade unions [being] *the* social movements"[12], the findings of this research reveal that the labour movement cannot adopt such a central position of rhetoric in its weakened state. Rather it must aim to develop organic networks with social movements and adopt their practices for the 21st century. Dynamism and flexibility held by other social movements are central requirements for the labour movement's development if it is to become an important part of GCS whose central characteristics and elements are hard to define, and interaction with other movements could allow the learning of these ways of operating.

Yet we must now assume that all within civil society are somehow inherently compatible with the labour movement or indeed each other. In turn it should be made explicit that a wide array of actors and ideas that are not necessarily compatible interact within this realm. Once we understand that GCS does not necessarily simply mean trusted global NGOs such as Greenpeace, we begin to uncover a fractious and contested nature of GCS that contrasts with simple conceptions of GCS as a homogenous entity

---

12. Interview with ICFTU Official, 2417/2002.

(Colas, 2002).

GCS does comprise many large, visible NGOs, but it also includes many divergent social associations, from local women's groups to anti-globalisation groups. As such GCS is open to challenges and conflict, and cannot be seen as a simple "bounded sphere" (Amoore and Langley, 2004, p93) operating alongside the political arena. Instead our very interpretation of what is meant by resistance is challenged as we see competing groups with differing agendas and plans congregating within an open socio-political space.

The openness and inclusivity that defines GCS can lead to an oversimplification of its components. Although "voluntary association" (Amoore and Langley, 2004, p94) is important it is similarly key that we do not simplify this further to assume it means a form of inherently 'good' politics. Such an equation of GCS and indeed traditional national level civil society with a somehow inherently 'good' form of action, as opposed to other realms such as that of the traditional state centered polity, which are deemed as 'bad'[13] would prove dangerous. This perception could lead to sets of actors and processes being "romanticised" (Pasha and Blaney,

---

13. Interview with ICFTU Official, 24 l 7/2002.

1998, p437) in a way that would mask conflict and division.

Despite discourse that "places it equally on the side of the angels" (Kaviraj and Khilnani eds. 2001, p153), GCS in reality has the potential to be a space within which for example "exclusionary populism" (Cox, 1999, p13) may prosper, just as much as free and co-operative socio-politics. If the labour movement is to create a form of counter-hegemonic movement or bloc, it is imperative that it pro-actively works against such a romanticisation without going so far as to demonise elements of GCS, in order that the correct and most effective linkages are made.

Recognising the divergence between those involved in GCS leads to a critical understanding of the concept, in which dangers of universalism are uncovered. To simply believe that one particular view of this global, social arena is correct for all contexts risks the creation of key problems where a certain western vision of a 'good' GCS is positioned in opposition to what may be a quite distinct, localised vision. This holds implications for the labour movement as efforts must be made to ensure that interests and issues facing workers around the world are recognised by those coordinating action within GCS, instead of imposing blanket values and standards on all groupings and individuals encountered.

Whilst actors within global civil society are for the most part striving for perceived positive societal change, there is a parallel process (which may be seen by some as 'bad') at work in which political and economic actors may attempt to co-opt GCS actors into their realm so that their actions are legitimated. Indeed it has been argued that GCS is "necessary to provide accountability in a system of global governance" (Amoore and Langley, 2004, p17) as a humane face is given to political and economic institutions. This caveat's importance is highlighted by the interaction between World Trade Organisation (WTO) and international labour organisations. For example, the latter were working to secure trading standards, only to find themselves in a position where success was minimal (Wilkinson and Hughes, 2000) but the capital body could argue that they had delivered a full social discussion.

One caveat that seems extreme if not simply misjudged is that many of the social movements that form GCS are mere irritants when judged from "the regal heights of statecraft" (Walker, 1994, p669). Whilst it is true that from the outside it may appear that formal economic and political institutions may have an inherent power lacking in social movements, their efficacy is based on social forces and agency and not realist power conceptions. Essentially GCS can be perceived in a variety of both positive and negative ways, but it is entirely wrong to negate its transformative power by arguing "global civil society is what states make of it" (Colas, 2002, p153). Instead it is more sensible to argue that GCS is what social movements make of it.

It is within this contested and debatable arena that the labour movement must attempt to internationalise and "reach out to other social movements" (O'Brien, 2000b, p515) so it may operate effectively in the 21st century (Moody, 1997). And today we are able to see certain elements of the labour movement, especially the ILO and WCL operating quite explicitly within GCS in order to promote the rights of workers. Indeed one of the ILO's founding principles embodies how civil society transcends national boundaries, as it argues "all human beings, irrespective of race, creed or sex, have the right to pursue both their material wellbeing and their spiritual development in conditions of freedom and dignity, of economic security and equal opportunity" (ILO, 2000e).

Pursuing such a trajectory provides the potential "for a restructuring of society and polity" (Cox, 1993, p272) in a way that allows an effective reaction to the global pressures of globalisation. Shifting downwards to lower levels of analysis, it appears that the globalisation of civil society means that national labour organisations need no longer fight in isolation for worker's rights, instead they are able to reach out as part of a larger coordinated whole, to link with others in a way that transcends national borders.

Integral to effective labour movement GCS engagement are efforts to work alongside Non-Governmental Organisations (NGOs) and social movements (ILO, 2000c). The ILO argues for a "continued and concerted international effort in which the representatives of workers and employers, enjoying equal status with those of governments, join with them [social movements] in free and democratic decision with a view to the promotion of the common welfare" (ILO, 2000c, pl). But the findings throughout this research highlight how this optimism for a "global solidarity" (Waterman, 1999b, pl) is not shared by all in the labour movement. At times it will be shown that "a new international labour movement...against a globalised, networked capitalism" (Waterman, 1999a, pl) is some way off.

Despite any scepticism shown, efforts within global civil society on the behalf of workers have the backing of the ILO with Juan Somavia (former Director General) arguing forcefully that "the absolute and concrete reality of the present is that the benefits of the global economy are not reaching enough people" (Somavia, 1999a, p 1), and the co-operation of divergent elements of a "global civil society" (Somavia, 1999a, p3) will play a large part in changing this. Later chapters will analyse the role the labour movement may have in this and to what extent the labour movement must change to meet contemporary challenges along the path laid out by social movement unionism.

Conclusion

This chapter has analysed the processes of globalisation and the challenges and opportunities they present to labour. Rather than looking at globalisation as a single phenomenon, four of the most important aspects of the process with regards to labour were explored. These are the globalisation of production, technology, governance and civil society. By looking at these intertwined aggregates of globalisation, issues were highlighted much more clearly than were a single, overarching concept of globalisation taken to be the focus of analysis.

In terms of the globalisation of production, the production structure (Strange, 1988) is dominated by large companies, many of which operate on a global scale. Companies have found themselves in a position where they can theoretically move operations when and where they like, and in doing so place many pressures on labour across the globe. The real picture however, is of companies perceived to be global and footloose that dominate the political economy around the world, and workers that are in need of an effective labour movement to challenge this dominance of capital.

Technology has allowed for the mechanisation of work within the context of the globalisation of production, both of which have led to an overall restructuring of what is meant by the term work (Hyman and Streeck, 1989). Whilst this means inevitably some labour is discarded, much human labour is still needed in both the developed and developing world. Thus, large numbers of workers finds themselves in a perilous position without social support or protection, a situation exemplified by looking at women's position within the world of work in the global age.

It is the labour movement as a whole that addresses these situations, and social movement unionism, with central principles of inclusivity and dynamism, presents the labour movement with a framework to recognise and address issues and workers currently outside its focus. Technology has however, also facilitated a communications revolution that has allowed labour organisations to co-operate and co-ordinate across territorial borders as a form of global civil society arises in response to changes in governance.

Governance has evolved and globalised in some respects as a response to and consequence of the processes of globalisation that make traditional, territorially orientated action less viable. We now see the development of supranational forms of governance that attempt to influence the global political economy in the same way as the nation state has in the past (O'Brien et al eds. 2000). Nevertheless, the nation state is still important, not least as the conduit through which legitimacy and support can be transferred to these supranational organisations.

If the labour movement were to remain entirely positioned at the national level then it would be outside the important frameworks for action in the modern global political economy. As part of a wide movement to develop a societal element to globalisation that has seen supranational forms of governance and capital prosper, civil society is globalising. Within this arena the labour movement can operate alongside fluid and dynamic social movements, and a key question for debate in this thesis is whether it is in a position to operate efficiently with such groupings, or indeed has the desire to do so.

The following chapter will build on this discussion of the challenges and potentials presented by globalisation to the labour movement. It will analyse the situation that faces the labour movement in Britain today, as this case presents a good picture of internal and external pressures in the national arena that have affected the labour movement. Critically there will also be a discussion of responses from British unions to the challenges that they face in all aspects of their contemporary operations, and to what extent these fulfil the remit of social movement unionism.

3. AN IPE OF BRITISH INDUSTRIAL RELATIONS

Introduction

The previous chapters provided a theoretical contextualisation for discussions of labour politics. The first chapter outlined how a Gramscian inspired theoretical framework provides suitable tools for understanding the world in which labour operates, whilst the concept of social movement unionism was argued to be an important tool to understand patterns of renewal within the labour movement. The second chapter moved to discuss globalisation and the key challenges and in some cases opportunities presented to the labour movement by globalising tendencies in production, technology, governance and civil society.

This chapter will build on the foundation provided by discussing the experiences of the British labour movement in modern times. Specifically it will analyse key features of the Conservative government of 1979-1997 and the 'New' Labour government post 1997 as it is argued that in these periods a concerted era of pressure was brought to bear on the labour movement, through processes of globalisation discussed in the previous chapter.

This national level of analysis forms part of a three level analysis, comprising the national, regional and global. It is necessary to look at developments at all of these levels as they intertwine - combining to provide the labour movement a complete framework in which to operate. In this sense the national dimension of analysis is one part of a wider contextualisation to arguments within the thesis. It provides the level at which a societal response to globalisation can be formed before it is shifted upwards and developed for the global level.

The initial section will provide a discussion of what has been termed the Thatcher project, a period of anti-union neo-liberal governance in Britain[14] that presented political, legal and social challenges to the labour movement (Edwards et al, 1998, pp 1-55). The second section argues that 'New Labour' Government pursued a strategy within British political economy that whilst being less neo-liberal, continued to marginalise trade unions (Gray, 1998). Such contextualisation and analysis allows for an understanding of the situation within which unions find themselves today in the UK, in turn providing broader insights into the national plights of workers across the globe. This is

---

14. Interview with TUC Official, 27/6/2002.

because the British labour movements' experience incorporates all the major challenges detailed in the previous chapter, in an often hostile and extreme manner.

Whilst British legislation during the last thirty years has often been anti-union, this is not the only reason for a loss of membership. It has been argued for example, that instead of a breakdown of all unionism, there has been a "crisis of a specific, narrowly based type of trade unionism" (Hyman and Ferner, 1994, pl13). If this is true, then a shift in focus beyond what are seen as traditional forms of labour movement in Britain towards more modern and dynamic organisations may bring benefits. In this sense social movement unionism presents a set of practices and indeed goals that the labour movement could strive for, including an incorporation of unprotected groups of labour that have previously been marginalised in the union agenda. It will be argued in this chapter that despite potential for renewal that the recruitment of workers including women and migrant workers, substantial stumbling blocks are still preventing such a course of action.

The next section moves to analyse whether British unions have seen fit to change their operating models in order to better face contemporary challenges. It will be argued that certain aspects of the social movement unionism framework are already being implemented, but in a relatively unorganised and haphazard way. The insights provided by this section will enable the research to show to what extent social movement unionism is being used within the labour movement in Britain as a means to reposition itself in the political economy not only of Britain but also of Europe and globally.

The Labour Movement and Neo-liberalism, 1979-1997

It has been argued that the period from the 1979 election of a Conservative government saw major changes in the British industrial relations landscape[15]. Amongst the key features of this period in British industrial relations are "the longest recorded decline in trade union membership and a fall in strike rates to their lowest ever levels [and] a decline in the role of collective bargaining" (Edwards et al, 1998, pi). So the position in which the labour movement of Britain finds itself today is made clear, it is important to understand what occurred in this period. Before embarking upon such analysis, some key characteristics that have

---

15. Examples of literature describing the period from 1979 in Britain
    .include Hyman and Ferner, 1994; Baglioni and Crouch, 1990; Marsh,
    1992; Ruysseveldt and VIsser, 1996; Ferner and Hyman, 1998.

historically marked the British trade union movement will be outlined so any observable changes are contextualised.

One key tradition within the pre-1979 British industrial relations system was the "handling of industrial relations at the level of the workplace" (Edwards et al, 1998, p3). Whilst in certain sectors of the economy there have in the past been industry level agreements (Marsh, 1990), there has been a tendency for rules of employment to be settled on a day-to-day basis within individual workplaces. This reflects a system relatively free of legal regulation or comprehensive high-level agreements, a trait that forms the second major tradition in British industrial relations.

A voluntaristic tradition in Britain saw the state as "remaining aloof from the process of collective bargaining in private industry. It left parties free to come to their own agreement" (Donovan, 1968, p 10), leading to a system of hands-off government with employers and employees free to reach compromise in disputes and negotiations. Within this framework the role of legislation was largely to provide exemptions from common laws that would render union organisation and action illegal, rather than specific legislation aimed to promote or hinder such activities (Brown et al, 1997, p2).

This relatively 'hands off approach to industrial relations

in Britain was challenged by the Conservative Government elected in 1979, whose anti-trade union legislation formed a key piece of its electoral programme. The Conservative government pursued a neoliberal agenda that saw the existing industrial relations system as "stifling managerial initiative and entrenching restrictive practices" (Brown et al, 1997, p3) necessary for economic progress in the modern age. There ensued a step-by-step passage of legislative reform of the British industrial relations system (Auerbach, 1990) that had a massive impact on the efficacy of trade unions to perform roles they had carried out in the past as it undercut their base[16]. From a peak position of power in 1970 when unions had 12,639,000 members and a labour force density of some 53.4%, by 2000 this had fallen to merely 7,295,000 union members representing a union density of 26% at the turn of the 21st century (Labour Market Trends, 2002, p344). Yet legislative reform in the quest for investment and economic growth and freedom was not the only challenge to the labour movement in this period.

The Conservative government came to power in a period of crisis for world capitalism that "necessitated a far reaching

---

16. Interview with TGWU Official, 9/9/2002.

restructuring of the economic, social and political conditions for capital accumulation" (Overbeeck and Van Der Pijl, 1993, p2). This was an organic crisis affecting all aspects of the global political economy that, it is argued, saw the breakdown of the "undisputed economic supremacy that the United States had enjoyed since the 1940s" (Gamble, 1988, p 1). There was a simultaneous breakdown of Fordism and at a national level in Britain, a breakdown of the "politics and institutions of post-war social democracy" (Gamble, 1988, p1). The political response to this crisis was the right wing neo-liberal agenda that had at its heart commitments to a free market society devoid of state intervention in the economy, and a strong state capable of preserving such a situation (Gamble, 1988; Waddington, 1992). Gradually this agenda became the hegemonic force in global politics as it was adopted in Britain, the United States and transferred to other countries around the world.

The collectivism that had developed in an era of Fordist mass production was challenged as "the scope of production was both reduced and made part of the global grid" (Overbeeck and Van Der Pijl, 1993, p17). The globalisation of technology and production discussed in the previous chapter combined to present governments with a vision of capitalism in which the labour movement was seen as an obstacle to progress (Waddington,

1992; Smith, 1999). Increased flexibilisation of labour, replacement of workers with technology, and globalised production may appear as organic developments that challenge the labour movement, yet they have in fact been promoted and supported by government policies that aimed to promote profit above social welfare and worker stability. Conservative government legislation sought to restrict "unions, strikes and collective bargaining, and to limit employee rights" (Van Ruysseveldt and Visser, 1996, p52) as barriers to economic growth and freedom were challenged. Such developments challenged the effectiveness and indeed relevance of traditional, institutionalised forms of worker organisation and representation in Britain.

Between 1979 and 1997 a raft of legislation was enacted that chipped away at what had previously been seen as fundamental union rights in Britain. Traditional forms of action such as picketing away from the primary workplace and secondary industrial action in the form of support for other workers were made illegal in most circumstances by the 1980 Act. A central element of this period of challenges to the labour movement was the effect of the ill-fated miners' strikes of the early 1980s.

In a fierce confrontation between trade unions and government, the opportunity was taken by the Conservative government to 'win the battle' with the trade union movement once and for all. Bitter confrontations on the streets came in a period that saw key Acts of Parliament in 1980, 82 and 84 that eventually meant "much of the existing statutory support for collective bargaining was dismantled" (Edwards et al, 1998, p14). Trade unions were increasingly seen as impediments to progress as militancy led at times to fierce violence and social upheaval, and as the government's ideology prevailed so a neo-liberal hegemonic bloc was built with the labour movement no longer amongst the "governing institutions" (Williams, 1997, p496). Instead as "union leaderships were excluded from any direct involvement in state bodies and agencies" (Fairbrother, 2000, p51), labour was cast as a "special interest group, representing a section of the community" (Fairbrother, 2000, p51) no longer central to society.

This British experience of globalised production and technology throughout this prolonged period, linked with the privatisation of national industries with strong union traditions, highlight the threats posed to workers and the labour movement as a whole. The increasing call for FDI from the British government did bring new companies and jobs, but these were often on the back of deals providing subsidies or union limiting agreements (Thomas, 1997). These developments reflect the challenges to the labour movement detailed in chapter two, and served to gradually weaken union numbers and leverage.

As new technologies and other elements of globalisation threatened the positions of workers, even those who found themselves in work were often the victims of moves towards "flexibilisation" (Marsh, 1992, p176) in the workplace. This process meant that the labour movement was hampered by lowering numbers of members, as part-time and temporary contract work replaced full-time employees who traditionally filled the ranks of unions. Simultaneously, moves towards increased employment within small workplaces and the service sector further threatened unions' position as these were areas of the economy that have long proven difficult to organise effectively (Ferner and Hyman, 1992).

During this period of challenges, the trade union movement appears to have failed to respond adequately to the pressures they faced[17]. Despite it being increasingly apparent that the traditional male, manufacturing class that formed the union base was being eroded, little was done to attract new constituent

---

17. Interview with TUC Official, 11/9/2002

members such as women and ethnic minorities (Kessler and Bayliss, 1998).There were few initiatives that would either engender wide support for their cause of protecting workers, or widen their membership to include growth areas of employment such as the service sector dominated by women[18]. Instead we can observe the crisis and erosion of a very particular male, manufacturing based unionism in large enterprises (Hyman and Ferner, 1994, p113) that is still affecting the labour movement today.

A key element of this period of British political economic history is its demonstration of the close linkages between national legislative developments and political-economic developments emanating from the external world. Whilst the "decline of trade union membership in Britain may not have been exceptional in international terms, the implications of it are" (Brown et al, 1997, p9), as a labour movement steeped in history and secure of its own position and importance was successfully sidelined by a neoliberal hegemonic government, focused on free market principles. The end of the Conservative Government's period of power thus saw a trade union movement

---

18. Interview with TUC Official, 1119/2002

ravaged by multiple factors that had affected them in the previous 20 years. A recasting of the global political economy in favour of a neo-liberal dominated agenda focused on free market principles (Overbeeck and Van der Pijl, 1993) had provided an economic and political context that fundamentally challenged the trade unions. Whilst the national political environment had been recast in an anti-union fashion as the government embraced the central processes of globalisation that were so challenging to the labour movement.

New Labour or No Labour?

Considering the traditional ideological differences between the Labour and Conservative parties of Britain, it could have been expected that the 1997 election victory by the Labour party could bring a new, more 'pro-labour' set of circumstances for the British labour movement. However, there was not a significant removal of legislation introduced between 1979 and 1997 that restricted the actions and efficacy of the labour movement in Britain (Smith and Morton, 2001; Gray, 1998), and linkages to the global arena of political-economics were just as important. It has been widely argued that 'New Labour' followed a path heavily influenced by the neo-liberal agenda pursued by the Conservatives (Undy, 1999;

Mclllroy, 1999), with a visible "substantive continuity with Tory policy in certain areas" (Gray, 1998, p1).

Within the first eighteen months of the Labour Government it appeared that policy was to be more pro-labour as Britain signed up to the Maastricht social policy, implemented a national minimum wage, and published proposals for new employment rights and statutory procedures for union recognition. The underlying reality is somewhat different however, as labour friendly legislation has been minimalist in form. An example of this apparent reluctance to commit fully to pro-labour policies is the implementation of the 1998 working time directive, a set of general statutory rules for the regulation of working time (Eiro, 1998a, p1).

This legislation was not necessarily the choice of the new government and was actually pushed upon New Labour following the European Court of Justice's (ECJ's) "rejection of the previous Conservative government's objection to its legal basis" (Undy, 1999, p327). That the implementation of this legislation was reluctant seems to highlight a prevailing propensity to satisfy employers rather than employees, as full use was made of any exceptions and derogations for sectors and professions available to them (Novitz, 2002).

Whilst not openly hostile to the labour movement, the Labour Government nonetheless seemed keen to pursue paths of action that did not harm the economic strength of the country at all costs. The adoption of a low minimum wage with rates starting from as low as £3.00 per hour (Undy, 1999, p327) shows that the labour movement still operated in a climate geared to be "as easy on employers as it could be"[19] (Smith and Morton, 2001, p123). It is weak legislation such as this that contributed to arguments that the Labour government was in fact attempting to "resist most attempts to improve social protection of labour" (Gray, 1998, pl). This perspective appears to be reinforced when one considers the sheer amount of anti-union legislation emanating from the Conservative government that remained in place. Despite the Prime Minister acknowledging that Conservative laws that "restrain access to industrial action" (Novitz, 2002, p505) were indeed "the most restrictive trade union laws in Europe" (Gray, 1998, p3), they remained in force.

Weakened by the challenges of the last twenty years the labour movement was and indeed remains unable to take advantage of opportunities that do present themselves. The 1999

---

19. Interview with GMB official, 12/9/2002.

Employment Relations Act that provided many individual, collective and family friendly employment rights was seen as "the most important and wide ranging piece of employment legislation in the UK for many years" (Eiro, 1999a, p2) was a missed opportunity. The labour movement was unable to win radical union recognition rights in its weakened position, and was instead forced to accept restrictive union recognition legislation that pertained only to workplaces with 21 or more employees, rather than including all businesses.

Because of this legislation, the labour movement had no binding legal right to organise some 31% of the workforce, a total of approximately 8.1 million workers (Simpson, 2000, p196). Even when the labour movement could attempt to organise workplaces, restrictions included pre-requisite support for the union in the workplace set at a level of "10% support in the relevant bargaining unit and that the majority of workers in that unit must favour recognition" (Novitz, 2002, p501). Rather than providing the labour movement with a strong legal base to begin a policy of repositioning global political economy, the situation was (and remains) that "ridiculously the union must have practically won the battle for recognition before it starts"[20].

With anti-union laws still remaining in force and the new legislation lacking in any real substantive gains for the labour movement, it can be argued that New Labour believed "unions ...act[ed] as a constraint upon the efficient operation of markets and individual freedom" (Smith and Morton, 2001, p120). And with Tony Blair himself stating that "there will be no going back...the days of strikes without ballots, mass picketing, closed shops and secondary action are over" (DTI, 1998, p3), the gauntlet was thrown down to the labour movement.

Instead of attempting to destroy unions as the Conservative government did, the Labour government appeared more at ease with attempting to subsume them within a form of social partnership. But the conception of partnership, which is at best a slippery subject, appeared to rely on pushing unions into a position where they would no longer be militant organisations but rather "co-operative and subordinate partners" (Smith and Morton, 2001, p121) to capital and government.

For the labour movement to successfully reposition itself along the path argued for by advocates of social movement

---

20. Interview with TGWU Official, 9/9/2002.

unionism, there has therefore long been a need for those in positions of power in Britain to "re-legitimise collectivism and reassert that the trade union movement has an essential role to play in national life" (McIllroy, 2000, p4). Despite the upbeat assertions of the Trades Union Congress (TUC) that the labour movement "wanted to share responsibility with government in making hard choices on key issues" (Financial Times, 30/911998) rather than descend into conflict, progress was limited. New Labour preferred to use unions "on a limited, *ad hoc* basis" (McIllroy, 2000, p4), which led to the labour movement remaining for the most part an ineffectual body largely disenfranchised from the mainstream political economy.

Whilst unions succeeded in attaining a certain air of legitimacy through appointments to government bodies such as that of Bill Morris of Transport and General Workers Union (TGWU) to the Council of the Bank of England, the all-important tripartite social partnership that the TUC saw as the future[21] seems unattainable. Attempts to create meaningful links to the Council for Business and Industry (CBI) ended in failure with the CBI "expressly opposed to ...ideas of social

---

21. Interview with TUC Official, 27/6/2002.

partnership" (Bacon and Storey, 2000, p410), explicitly stating that whilst they remained open to ad hoc consultation and joint goals, they "had no interest in institutionalised partnership" (Mclllroy, 2000, p6).

With at least certain unions historically recognising the usefulness of "hard bargaining and calculative militancy" (Kelly, 1996, pl00), it is necessary to discuss whether the British labour movement has attempted to pursue social movement unionism to reposition itself, or whether there are particular stumbling blocks in the way of this policy. Fast forward to 2018 and Trade Unions remain in a type of limbo. Not able to operate in partnership with government of big business, but not quite adapting their methods to move beyond traditional strikes. The answer to gain influence has appeared at least to centre on gaining political traction within the latest iteration of the Labour Party. 'Old-style' industrial action affecting sectors such as Higher Education and public transport have been joined by increasingly close relationships with left-leaning post-Blair Labour leaders. But does this really make any difference to workers in the real world?

British Social Movement Unionism

According to the debate surrounding social movement unionism, the British labour movement, like so many others, found (and finds) itself at a crossroads where a path towards renewal and response to recent pressures can be embarked upon. This section will discuss two broad strands of action debated within the labour movement. First, changes to the structures of unions in terms of membership and recruitment, and second, changes to the practices carried out by unions such as organising members and forging links to other social movements.

In a sense these two elements of change are intertwining and reinforcing, but it is not immediately clear whether progress towards one will inevitably lead to progress in the other. Although it does seem relatively likely that were institutional changes to be implemented successfully, changes in attitude and action may well follow as previous procedures and norms would no longer be viable. In analysing these policies it will be shown that social movement unionism has been pursued in an ad-hoc and haphazard way. Fearful of wholesale changes yet recognising the need for new developments, the British experience is one of being 'caught between two stools' in the quest for renewed influence and power.

For unions to become more central to the running of the

British political economy, proponents of social movement unionism argue that moves must be made to effectively organise and recruit more "nonstandard" (Jenson et al, 2000, p6) workers. This call comes as prevailing pressures have forced a decline in traditional industries that provided union members, newer service industries less likely to unionise have come into prominence. Such a shift has severely affected unions, historically focused on what may be described as 'traditional' forms of full time, often manufacturing type workplaces and workers (Kessler and Bayliss, 1998).

Central to the new constituencies of workers highlighted as important for unions are women, whilst migrant and ethnic minority workers are also often outside union remits. But since some 90% of the new jobs created in services sectors since 1970 in Britain alone have gone to women (Whittock, 2000, p146), this is a logical focus for the labour movement's attentions. Mirroring the increasing importance in formerly ignored groups of workers, is the increasing importance of part time and temporary workers as discussed in chapter three, meaning that differing forms of employment as well as workers are to be addressed by trade unions.

There are examples of unions apparently shifting their methods of operating in order that such challenges are addressed, however. An 'off the record' discussion with a union official told of a case in a North of England British Airways call centre that had one single union member in the early 2000's. This member then brought to the attention of the union not only the key issues which may prompt workers to unionise, but also detailed reports of which workers could be receptive to the union's position. By making contact with colleagues within the workplace, the union member was able to ascertain differing people's attitudes and aspirations, in turn deciding which would be most amenable to joining the union. Simultaneously information was relayed to the union itself on what ground-level workers thought of the organisation, and what issues they held as being most important. Such skillful, grassroots organisation led to an eventual total of over 200 workers becoming unionised and the employer being placed in a position where it had no option but to agree to union recognition for collective agreements.

By shifting operations, at least in this one instance, away from a grand level of socio-politics towards the lowest levels of action, the union was presenting a test for neo-Gramscian assumptions. Focusing on social linkages at a low level, before shifting the challenge upwards, meant attention was being paid to possibly more coherently developing a process of building resistance. This appears to be indicative of new practices that "focus on the employment interests of workers and almost exclusively have been developed at workplace and company levels" (Heery, 2002, p27), even if the language and policy behind it is contrary to the new social movement unionism in its out-dated and ad hoc appearance.

It seems somewhat artificial to separate the issues of female work and part time work, as figures show 44% of all female work being part-time as opposed to 8% of male work (Thair and Risdon, 1999, p104). This leads to the description of part-time work as a "female ghetto" (Jenson et al, 1998, p7). Yet with certain figures within the labour movement arguing that "part time and women workers (the two equate to each other) are vital for the future"[22], it is still questionable whether adequate steps have been taken to bring them into the movement's remit. One impediment to the incorporation of excluded workers into the British labour movement appears to be a lack of understanding as to the composition of social groupings outside the traditional focus of the labour movement.

It is important that an acknowledgement of the multi-faceted nature of societal groups is retained; yet at times this is

---

22. Interview with ICGLTW Official, 7/8/2002.

lacking in union perspectives. It is problematic to retain a view that workers of any sort somehow have an automatic homogeneity, given the multiplicity of circumstances encountered by women such as economic status, marital status, education and whether they have children or not (Waylen and Randall, 1998). The union officials interviewed in this research appeared to retain such a homogenous view however, and pointed towards the existence of identifiable "common concerns" (Parker, 2000, p24) within these groups that are actually as divergent as any other element of society.

Regardless of whether the labour movement wishes to recruit new workers simply to boost numbers or to begin a path of radical development geared towards the contemporary political economy, the trend to see groups as a homogenous whole appears to be stifling attempts. This has meant that whilst some may acknowledge the importance of recruitment, because of lack of understanding unions "have not been sympathetic to their needs" (Walters, 2002, p52). Ignorance of circumstances and perspectives has at times led to a situation where "women workers [were seen as a] challenge and a threat to male workers who were members" (Donaghy, 1995, p179) of unions.

Such narrow and mistaken attitudes appear to be

receding[23], yet the policies being implemented at the ground level within unions to attract groups of female and part time workers remain somewhat low-key and non-strategic. The attitude of a TGWU official was that attracting women was historically based around appearing too masculine, although it might just be "too difficult"[24] to attract workers currently outside the union movement, due to obstacles in gaining access to them such as time constraints, travel issues and issue surrounding the form of work carried out by workers. In this sense attitudes rather than tangible issues appear to be hindering the development of an inclusive labour movement as token efforts are made to placate critics. With both institutional and attitudinal changes both being insufficient to engender any meaningful change in the union.

The true obstacles that lie in the path of recruiting women workers include irregular shift patterns and short shifts incurred with part-time work that may stop contact being made with officials. Whilst simultaneously women may often be employed in the service sector that has developed devoid of union presence due to the legislative and socio-political background of the last

---

23. Interview with GMB Official, 27/5/2002
24. Interview with TGWU Official, 9/9/2002.

20 years (Kessler and Bayliss, 1998). Ground level activities such as the contacting of ethnic minority workers with union members from their own backgrounds may help secure the trust and eventual membership of some workers, but they do not address the deeper traditions and practices that permeate unions. This means that for the most part British unions remain in essence white, male dominated arenas that are apparently exclusive to those outside them. Strategies such as providing "very good television adverts"[25] appear to have taken precedence over more deep seated changes to concrete structures, or engrained attitudes held by union officials.

It is therefore debatable whether attempts at recruitment of new groups will have an impact on the prevailing structures or practices within the unions. Merely by having women, part time workers and ethnic minorities within union ranks does not mean that the unions will necessarily become more feminised or racially aware (Donaghy, 1995, p192; Cook et al, 2000). Even when new workers are attracted to unions, there is often not an accompanying acknowledgement that these workers share the same fears and pressures as full time workers, yet also have their own set of circumstances that must be addressed such as the need

25. Interview with UNISON Official, 9/9/2002.

for equal legal rights and fair pay (Shaw and Perrons, 1995). Simultaneously, "unless structures are created which ensure the full participation of' women and ethnic minorities at all levels in the trade unions (Donaghy, 1995, p192), it is unlikely that the agenda or practices of the union will develop and we will witness the mere 'tacking on' of women to the labour movement instead. Instead a combination of shifts in attitude must be complemented by changes in structures, for without enabling mechanisms, new members and ideas are meaningless, yet without the latter, new structures are without any real worth.

To an extent unions have made efforts at resolving the issue of representing differing social groupings across different union levels through the use of reserved seats and dedicated groupings. Where we see "positive action strategies" (Healy and Kirton, 2000, p343) that reserve seats on union panels and boards from the bottom to the very top levels, it is guaranteed that women become prominent and influential. This is an attempt to counteract the situation whereby the influx of groups such as "women into workplaces and unions has not translated into equivalent increases in their opportunities, position and power in unions" (Parker, 2002, p23). Some unions such as the Public Services Union (UNISON) and the TGWU also have reserved seats on high level committees for black workers, but this in itself portrays an ignorance on behalf of unions as to the true multi ethnic nature of society as there is the omission of Asian, Latin and Middle Eastern workers to name but a few minorities not covered by the term 'black'. The argument from unions seems to be that positive action for some more visible elements of society in the promotion of inclusivity is better than none.

Another strategy for empowering marginalised elements of society within unions has been the creation of women and black groups influenced by the TUC's strategy of increasing representation of these groups within labour organisations and in the workplace (www.TUC.org/law). These operate based on a belief that by organising as a coherent group, societal elements will be able to address common concerns as "there are issues that bear more on them as a disadvantaged group" (Parker, 2000, p24). With an aim that the wider union agenda may in time be influenced by the arguments and thoughts of these groups, they "use their agency to inject their own beliefs, values and concerns into strategy and action" (Kirton and Greene, 2002, p160). Such developments seem to be more strategic than other campaigns, and could conceivably lead to changes in the attitudes held by unions as a whole organisation, yet they cannot redevelop the labour movement on their own. To believe that they can do is to reject the multi-faceted approach to change presented by social movement unionism.

The British trade union movement cannot simply rely on structural changes such as recruiting new members, in the hope that the very fabric of the organisations will in turn be changed. Instead a comprehensive reform agenda would include the development of more militant unionism, less concerned with providing health cover, with increased links to other social movements as well as the development of a more transnational nature (Waterman, 1998). Social movement unionism, as discussed previously, has as part of its doctrine an advocacy of moves towards more ground level "adversarial politics" (Heery, 2002, p27), which emphasises plurality, rather than the search for simplistic homogenous groupings or perspectives.

Through the measures discussed above, it appears that unions have attempted to implement such policies to a degree, but the following sections will discuss whether attitudes regarding union relations with outside elements has changed in recognition that capital and labour are not necessarily natural bedfellows, "as partnership unionism implies no single relationship with union members, so organising implies no single pattern of interaction with employers" (Heery, 2002, p28).

Perhaps the most striking change within union practices in Britain has been a shift away from 'servicing' members through means of economic facilities, towards an emphasis on 'organising' workers so that they may more effectively fight for their rights (Mclllroy, 2000, p2). This is an example of a shift towards ground level initiatives, with which the labour movement can attain "effective workplace organisation that can reproduce and service itself and provide a channel for the continuing recruitment of new employees in the union" (Heery, 2002, p28) as relevancy is given to the union.

A TGWU official described what this new developing form of unionism meant for him and his organisation, arguing that by developing a "ground level, shop floor unionism"[26] such as that discussed above with regards to the call centre recruitment, union members become more effectively represented by others who have real life experiences of the issues that matter. Yet this very statement of the term 'shop- floor' shows the difficulty in moving on from past conceptions, as it is a value laden concept that appears to exclude new forms of work such

26. Interview with TGWU Official, 9/9/2002.

as home-base working, or call centre work from its understanding of the union's remit. Such a tension highlights the relatively unplanned nature of developments, yet some implementations of such policies do appear to be gaining successes.

Whilst developments such as these seem to allow for the recognition of workers immediate concerns and wishes (Carter and Poynter, 1999), they are not necessarily as deep rooted or militant as the aims of social movement unionism. Upon questioning, officials from GMB and UNISON said that militancy is still very much 'watered down' due to the remaining legislative pressures that hinder effective strike action.[27].Whilst it is true that much of the 'anti-union' legislation enacted by the Conservative government remains in place (Gray, 1998, p1), a negative attitude exists in the labour movement that hampers the dynamic attitude alluded to in the foundations of this research.

The American union movement, which has operated for years within an extremely hostile environment has used social movement unionist principles much more fully and effectively

---

27. Interviews with GMB Official, 27/5/2002 and UNISON Official, 9/9/2002

than their British counterparts, and shows that British unions need to take a more wide-ranging view of the actions available to them. The American Federation of Labor-Congress of Industrial Organizations (AFL-CIO) has pioneered non-strike based actions such as sit-ins at restaurants to highlight issues for concern without breaking or challenging laws (Mort, 1998), alongside 'organising' based unionism that ensures unions address issues that "directly affect [workers] on the job" (Mort, 1998, pl16). This shows the effectiveness of pursuing policies of change in direct relation to each other, at the ground level such as was the case with the call-centre recruitment, as oppose to the rather ad-hoc manner that seems to prevail across most of the British experience.

The move towards a form of social movement coalition through increased linkages between the labour movement and other social groups (Munck, 1998, p9) is another element of social movement unionism that has not been fully incorporated into British trade unionism either through structural or attitudinal change.

Interviews with union officials suggest that the British experience of social coalition is fractured and minimalist at best. Whilst it is argued that increased linkages to other social movements on behalf of unions is a "big debate"[28], there is a reluctance to fully embrace any developments that would broaden the remit of the labour movement.

It was argued that the core business of the TUC was to represent employees with respect to employers and whilst they may at times go beyond that narrow remit, the focus was very much still on the core ethos of workplace relations[29]. This position seems myopic, especially when it is increasingly argued that workers have long been affected by issues not only in the workplace, but also outside by everyday issues such as the environment to racism (ICFTU, 2000) due to their position within the all-encompassing social relations of production. Yet still the labour movement has historically appeared uneasy with such a conception, with the TGWU stating quite categorically that any links to other social movements should "pertain to the world of work and nothing more"[30]. Hostile and defensive attitudes towards change such as this appear to show that regardless of any structural or practical changes, attitudes are perhaps the most important part of change.

---

28. Interview with TUC Official, 27/6/2002.
29. Interview with TUC Official, 27/6/2002.
30. Interview with TGWU Official, 9/9/2002.

But what exactly is the world of work envisaged by this element of the labour movement? The position of remaining bound to a rather confusing and ill- defined conception of the union remit was explained informally, as an attempt by the union to show workers and employers that it is really focused on where money was made or lost for workers. There appeared to be a concern that were they seen to invest effort in other areas of action, then members would fear they would not be as effectively protected. Yet there are already large numbers of workers outside the labour movement's boundaries. Issues such as homeworking, unpaid work, gender and race issues in society as a whole and in the workplace, all combine to make the world of work a far-reaching and contested concept (Whittock, 2000, p1). And the tension between this inclusive approach and the narrow conception often held by unions shows once again the fractured and flawed fashion in which union policies are developed.

As well as a myopic view of the union remit, there has been scepticism as to the merits of many potential social partners within civil society that would serve to broaden the labour movement's perspective. One official argued that unions were "very cynical towards social movements, there is lots of 'using' of parties going on and woolly political correctness that doesn't really help the representation of workers"[31]. This highlights an apparent fundamental lack of trust on the part of unions when discussing social movements. Much was made in interviews conducted of the need for unions to be sure of the true motives of other groups, and the fact that unions and observers should be aware of "differing agendas"[32] that could jeopardise permanent partnerships between social movements.

There was also at times an appearance of 'aloofness' on the part of unions who seem to value above all the "democratic accountability"[33] of trade unions that they feel other social movements lack, a stance that apparently ignores the fact that many of the democratic controls within unions were imposed from above through restrictive Conservative legislation. In this sense other social movements are seen as somehow less trust worthy, as in many cases they do not have the same traditional institutionalised structures and procedures as unions. Yet this is an implicit rejection of the call within social movement unionism to shift operations away from rigid structures towards more fluid and dynamic ways of operating more suitable to the modern age

---

31. Interview with TGWU Official, 9/9/2002
32. Interview with Unison Official, 9/9/2002.
33. Interview with TUC Official, 27/6/2002.

(Munck, 1998). Again, even if structural changes brought about linkages to other movements, it is doubtful given prevailing attitudes whether these would be successful.

Cynicism does not completely dominate the labour movement in Britain, and the GMB in particular seemed eager to address issues other than traditional work related ones, attempting as they are to operate with groups "at every level global, regional national, and sub regional and community"[34]. It was argued that by developing links to other societal groupings the union would "become part of the community rather than being a stand-offish organisation"[35]

This points towards the internationalist arguments that underpin this research, with the aim of repositioning labour as a truly transnational actor in the same sense as transnational capital (Waterman, 1999a, pl). With globalisation identified as the "key agenda for the future"[36] for trade unions even by national figures, and the recognition that unions are acting within "European and global Markets which affect people's

---

34. Interview with GMB Official, 27/5/2002
35. Interview with GMB Official, 27/5/2002
36. Interview with TGWU Official, 9/9/2002

lives"[37] there seems at least an initial acknowledgement that simply operating alone within defined borders will impair the effectiveness of British trade unions.

An observable aspect of a growing internationalisation within some British unions is an agenda of co-operation and co-ordination with other national trade unions around the world. The GMB exemplify this through their linkages to organisations involved not only in labour issues but also wider humanitarian issues as far afield as Haiti. Other unions such as UNISON have pursued similar policies, choosing to foster links to European unions involved in similar sectors of the political economy of their particular country.

Such programs of unity seem to provide a sense of the unions operating within a greater body than its own, meaning that they acknowledge that the modern pressures facing workers cannot adequately be addressed through geographically limited processes. The comparative eagerness of unions to pursue this line of action as opposed to others above may be explained by the fact that very little internal changing of either structures or attitudes is necessary for success. Communication and co-operation with other groups that can lend advice, support and

37. Interview with GMB Official, 27/5/2002

ultimately leverage in the global political economy does not necessarily involve a shifting of attitudes or changes in embedded structures in the same way as incorporating more divergent groups of workers, or acting in a more dynamic and militant fashion.

The European dimension of the political economy of Britain has often been seen as key for labour, as the TUC argued: "all the good labour stuff comes from Europe"[38]. Indeed, the social dimension of European integration presents the labour movement with such opportunities for positive legislation that it is argued: "the TUC now relies on the European level to push labour policies and initiatives through at the national level. ..[and that] all social elements of politics in Britain now come from Europe"[39]. If this is the case then analysis of the existing linkages and structures existing at the European level will give insight into the potential for the labour movement to challenge the hegemonic order effectively above the national level. Yet for British unions apparently keen to internationalise, the ETUC (the peak level European labour organisation) seems somewhat irrelevant.

---

38. Interview with TUC Official, 27/6/2002.
39. Interview with TUC Official, 27/6/2002.

On the one hand Brexit promises a range of challenges to link the national level to European bodies. Be it through the exit of the UK from key legislation or executive bodies, or mere practical issues around the movement of people, good s and services. But on the other hand past experience has led to a sense of division between the national and EU levels. The latter could be explained as the ETUC pursues a rather formalised and 'long-winded' approach to action, with officials dealing with national TUCs who must in turn discuss issues with their national union members before workers see results, meaning in essence that individual unions and workers are "divorced"[40] from the ETUC, with issues taking too long to filter down to the ground level.

Yet this should not explain a complete neglect of the importance of the European institutions that exist. For as has already been acknowledged by some within the British labour movement, "all the power is already in Europe"[41] – and has been for some time. With this in mind the next chapter will analyse the differing structures that exist at the European level, and will discuss what has held back effective internationalising of the

40. Interview with ETUC Official, 22/7/2002

41. Interviews with GMB Official, 27/5/2002 and UNISON Official, 9/9/2002

labour movement at the regional level.

Conclusion: Fractured British Social Movement Unionism?

This chapter has analysed the experiences and reactions of British trade unions over two key periods – the Conservative and Labour governments of the 1980's, 1990's and 2000's. By looking at the intertwined pressures of legislation and globalisation placed on the labour movement during the Conservative government of 1979-1997, it highlighted the constraining and difficult context which unions found themselves operating within. The labour movement did not adequately react to these legal and economic pressures (Fairbrother, 2000, pp47-49) and eventually found themselves with vastly reduced membership figures as well as weakened bargaining powers and leverage within the political economy of Britain. When the Labour Party was elected to power in 1997, hopes were high that many of the prevailing restrictions on union activity would be removed and that this could provide unions with an impetus for renewal (Kelly, 1997). This was not the case however and it has been argued that New Labour actually pursued a modified neo-liberal agenda that led to the continuance of unions being regarded as 'second class citizens'.

This means that over time unions have been forced to look for new ways to address the pressures they face in order that they are able to renew. Key elements from the social movement unionism discussed in chapter one and analysed the extent to which British unions have implemented these policies of development in their remit. It has become apparent that many of the trade unions in Britain are actually already pursuing policies for renewal that share influences with social movement unionism, but the necessary combination of changes to structures and practices, alongside shifts in attitudes has yet to materialise.

Instead policies of redevelopment appear on the whole to be somewhat fractured in their formulation and implementation, whilst there appears very little or no co-ordination being taken between national unions who face the same pressures. Scepticism was widely shown by many involved in unions towards most aspects of change, not least the fostering of links to other social movements and investing time and efforts into institutional European labour politics. Instead there existed some individual cases of working with certain groups and other country's unions on an apparent ad-hoc basis, developments that remain exceptional and unlikely to become the absolute norm unless wide ranging changes are brought about. With regards to new forms of organising and recruitment the picture was very similar, with unions pursuing divergent means of working towards the same goals of invigoration and renewal, with attitudes often being hostile to new practices, and structural/institutional changes being someway short of complete redevelopment.

There is a need for British unions to undertake much more structured and comprehensive paths of development as outlined by the social movement unionism model. But to do so successfully and comprehensively means that a sense a contradiction at the heart of new social movement unionism, which is exemplified by the British case, will have to be addressed. This contradiction is that the embracing of a social movement ethos of fluidity and issue-based action seems at times to be an anathema to organisations who are precisely seeking to define themselves in terms of membership and the notion of the 'shop-floor'.

Until this contradiction of institutionalisation and traditional values meeting dynamism and movement is addressed, it will prove problematic for the labour movement to pursue a policy of change that adequately addresses the challenges they face. Theorists argue that unions must work together and unite in order that skills are experiences are shared, and they must simultaneously undertake similar moves with other social groups and foreign bodies (Cox, 2000, p29). This process could lead to an internationalised, representative and efficient labour movement more suited to the challenges that have built up in the last 30 plus years. Yet such a process could be more successful if there are in place already supranational frameworks that can provide assistance and facilitate renewal. With this in mind the research will now move to analysing the existing labour movement structures that exist at the European level, and what if anything is hampering the internationalisation of the labour movement.

4. A DEVELOPING EUROPEAN SOCIAL MOVEMENT UNIONISM?

Introduction

One of the conclusions of the previous chapter, which analysed developments affecting the British labour movement, was that a developed and coherent European dimension to the labour movement could help moves towards social movement unionism. This chapter will analyse the labour movement frameworks that exist at the European level and assess to what extent they are facilitating the shifting of operations upwards from the national level in order to better compete with contemporary international capital (Taylor and Mathers, 2002). As it has been argued that the future success and survival of the labour movement depends upon "the extent to which the unions succeed in shedding the national constraints of their organisational structures and areas of action and internationalising them, and the extent to which opportunities and new organisational potentials are exploited" (Hoffman and Hoffman, 2001, p6).

This chapter will analyse the European Trade Union Confederation (ETUC) and assess whether it could represent an element of a broader social movement unionism. The ETUC, set up with aims to "internationalise the trade unions in Europe" (Oesterheld and Olle, 1978, p206) presents a vision of a centralised form of labour organisation, and it will be asked whether this model is effective in the modern political economy.

European Industry Federations (EIFs) also come under scrutiny in light of the ETUC's decision to pursue at the European level "a policy of co-ordinated bargaining in which the EIFs have the prime responsibility for the co-ordination function" (Waddington, 2001, p460). This could conceivably facilitate the industry level becoming central to the European labour movement (Le Queux and Fajertag, 2001). The final form of labour institution to be analysed are European Works Councils (EWCs), company based cross border structures that represent workers representation (Lecher and Rub, 1999) that appear to present a relatively low level of action in European industrial relations.

Throughout the analysis of these institutional frameworks for the Europeanisation of industrial relations', the research will critically analyse any progress being made towards the goal of a supranational labour movement. In doing so it will determine the extent to which the central conditions necessary for a successful Europeanisation of the labour movement are being met.

These central elements are argued to be the presence of viable and willing employer groups with which the labour movement can work, and a shift away from reliance on political figures and institutions for the delivering of conditions and policies that facilitate labour movement action. Integral to this last point is a need to build popular support for the Europeanisation process and the European level organisations that exist.

Central to delivering these conditions are the needs for attitudinal and structural changes within the labour movement at this level as well as at the national level, particularly towards more inclusive and co-operative ways of operating. With this in mind the chapter will then move to discuss how prevailing attitudes within the European level of the labour movement show a disregard for moves to co-operation and co-ordination with other social movements. This apparent rejection of social movement unionism mirrors many opinions shown at the national level, and threatens the potential that exists for a renewed focus for supranational level operations that would be of importance for workers across the region.

Conditions for the Europeanisation of Social Movement Unionism

The labour movement at the European level has found itself marginalised throughout the development of the EU, with legislation serving to "extend the markets in which trade unions were operating and transferred significant regulatory authority from national to European institutions" (Dolvik, 1997, p 1). Yet, such changes were imposed upon the labour movement without complementary or simultaneous developments in the societal dimension of integration. Essentially the labour movement within Europe remained rooted at the national level whilst political-economic power and influence was shifted up to the regional level. This means that workers within Europe have been and are still lacking protection and organisation that matches supranational capital, as "social integration is still lagging behind economic integration" (Keller and Bansbach, 2001, p432).

The Social Protocol, first annexed to the Maastricht treaty, aimed to combat this shortfall by making social dialogue more central, as social partners were given "not only the opportunity of informal hearings, but the right to voluntarily conclude binding framework agreements" (Keller and Bansbach, 2001, p420). This was designed to replace what has been coined the "Val- Duchesse dialogue" (Terry and Towers, 2000) whereby European level peak organisations of labour and capital participated in European social policy formation through voluntary and non-binding agreements (Martin and Ross, 1999) that has hampered the ability of the European labour institutions to appear effective and legitimate. Even with positive moves, European workers still find themselves represented by national based systems attempting to influence developments occurring away from "the nation state that trade unions have traditionally sought and achieved considerable influence" (Waddington and Hoffman, 2000, p28).

A critical step towards developing social movement unionism at the European level is the engagement of popular support for the project at the national and local levels from trade unions and their members. With trade unions seemingly keen to remain focused on problems at the national level, there has been "little popular interest in international solidarity" (Turner, 1996, p326). "Widespread fears...that the unions' influence and room for manoeuvre could be restricted" (Waddington and Hoffman, 2000, p629) by a shifting of powers and procedures above the national level appear to halt the development of an international dimension to the labour movement. National industry unions see any moving of collective bargaining or decision making as a zero sum game.

It is argued that national trade unions are facing a situation where the "diminishing role and authority" (Goetschy, 1996, p262) they have faced in recent times can be effectively addressed by moves towards increased internationalism. Yet, such a shift in policy can only be made acceptable to national figures and organisations through the facilitating actions of those involved in the European dimension of the labour movement. The ETUC has potential in this sense as an organising and networking centre, but is fighting against the conceptions held by national figures that "Europe to a great extent doesn't matter"[42]. Only by pursuing a policy of engendering popular support, engaging effectively with other societal actors and shifting away from relying on political favours towards multi- level action, can the Europeanisation of the labour movement succeed.

The ETUC and EIFs present structures that have the potential to provide at least the starting point for a European labour movement, yet attitudinal and structural changes seem necessary before this becomes a reality. National level organisations must commit themselves to co-operation and internationalisation as discussed in the previous chapter, but

---

42. Interview with GMB Official, 27/5/2002

impetus could be lent to such action by a proactive ETUC. By moving away from a vision of the ETUC as a supranational congress, and more towards a dynamic central hob of a European wide labour movement, the ETUC may present a more amenable vision of Europeanisation to national bodies. Doing so would in turn facilitate the effective European wide development of unions along social movement unionist lines, as experiences and attitudes are exchanged, with a broadening of remit occurring through increased linkages to other social movements. In this sense the ETUC is well placed to become a central part of a dynamic labour movement, acting as a facilitator for co-operation, and organiser of information exchange rather than simply as a political lobbyist. If a policy of co-ordination and dynamism was coupled with a commitment to the redevelopment of the labour movement as a whole, the ETUC could highlight the possibilities for the effective internationalisation of the movement across the globe, built upon contemporary principles of social movement unionism.

Beneath this peak organisational framework, EIFs have a role to perform as essentially transnational trade unions, co-ordinating dispute action and negotiations with organisers and employers around the region. Yet within a fluid and dynamic labour movement they also fill a position as intermediaries between the ETUC and national bodies, as their ties to both sides position them to facilitate exchanges of information and policy from the ETUC downwards. With the ETUC almost acting as a 'think tank' and network centre, EIFs in this sense fulfil a role of coordinating tangible social movement unionism at the ground level EWCs simultaneously take on a role as ground level bases for the development of action less reliant on institutional procedures and more on up to date information exchanges (Lecher and Rub, 1999, p8).

These developments have the potential to build a "representational base or mobilisational constituency" (Taylor and Mathers, 2002, p97) that is necessary for the Europeanisation of the labour movement. But with political structures existing at the European level, and a goal being the Europeanisation of the labour movement, it is at least desirable that there is a credible and willing employer organisation in order that the labour movement may aspire to enter into true binding social European dialogue (Degryse, 2002, p5) when necessary. Without such an opponent it is entirely conceivable that the labour movement will be unable to enter into discussions that have meaningful outcomes for workers as ultimately all decisions rely on political will from above. It is such a reliance on political will from above that is to be rejected if social movement unionism, with its emphasis on societal change through the actions of social agents, is to be achieved. In a sense the three prerequisites of shifts in attitudinal and structural norms leading to ease of action and increased popular support, movement away from reliance on political favours, and the need for credible employer counterparts are intertwining and self-reinforcing. In order to guarantee success in the Europeanisation project it is necessary that all of these conditions are met, and not just one of them individually, and in tum it appears that the most critical condition is a move to gain popular support (Gobin, 1994, p270).

A Centralised Framework for European Industrial Relations?

The ETUC, founded in 1973, seems on first analysis to present a viable opportunity to represent "the interests of wage earners in relations with the institutions of the European community" (Oesterheld and Olle, 1978, p211). Yet the ETUC has yet to fulfil its potential, having as it does within its organisational remit a confusing combination of national union congress', Interregional Trade Union Committees (ITUCs) and more recently EIFs (Groux, Mouriaux and Pemot, 1993). Transparency is not aided by the fact that the ETUC shares a Secretary General with a Pan-European Regional Council (a European trade union organisation within the ITUC, comprising 87 national trade union bodies).

Beyond such a lack of clarity, a central problem has been that social dialogue at the European level has not been organic, but has to a great extent relied on the European Commission that presented the social face of Europeanisation (Groux et al, 1993). In essence the ETUC is therefore a social partner with no organic support in the form of member workers who may lend their social agency to a particular cause, and is instead an organisation built on political support, from the top-down. Indeed the ETUC owes its very existence not to a groundswell of European worker power, but to the Delors led Commission that not only made "social dialogue an explicit Community objective" (Martin and Ross, 1997, p 13) but also "supplied money to fund ETUC' s internal activities" (Martin and Ross, 1997, p15).

Historical political support does not secure the success for a labour movement however. Social movement unionism as discussed in this research also promotes ground level, militant action as a way of operating in the modern age, and to rely on external organisations, particularly political organisations, appears to be a rejection of such a dynamic strategy. By relying on institutional norms and values the ETUC appears more as a tool of the polity than a representative organisation for workers in need of protection that new social movement unionism calls for, and there is a pressing need for the ETUC to look towards engaging the support of workers at the ground level in order that it may become more of a social movement.

Due to its precarious position as a serious social actor[43,] the ETUC has long been resigned to conducting little more than "non-committal fireside chats between management and labour" (Hoffman, 2000, p640). The will of European Commissions that were in favour of a societal dimension to European integration could only ever push the process so far, and more binding processes have been supported by few outside the ETUC. Indeed without explicit intervention from political institutions, dialogue between the ETUC, the Union of Employers' Confederations of Europe (UNICE) and the European Centre for Public Enterprises (CEEP) have often merely led to a "series of joint opinions and similar declarations on different topics" (Keller and Bansbach, 2001, p421). And whilst the ETUC may have favoured more binding

---

43. This insight comes from personal correspondence with Dr Peter Waterman, 11/9/2002

results, economic 'partners' such as UNICE have historically been in favour of keeping substantive processes at the national level (Keller and Bansbach, 2001, p421). It therefore appears that for some time the pinnacle organisation of the European labour movement was sidelined by other socio-political agents unwilling to co-operate, and as having no clear policy for addressing the issue in a dynamic and contemporary fashion.

The Maastricht Treaty that accorded the provision for peak socio-economic bodies to be formally recognised in social discussions at the European level, seems to have been an opportunity for the labour movement to secure a central position within the political economy of Europe. Yet despite optimism on behalf of the ETUC that progress could be attained in the field of "getting the goods for workers"[44], this has been difficult to live up to. Even with apparent success in securing legislation on parental leave, part-time work and fixed term contracts between 1995 and 1998, there has still been a reliance on political rather than popular will to push through proposals.

A fundamental change in focus appears necessary if the ETUC is to move away from reliance on political favours and instead to develop into a central European organisation of any

44. Interview with ETUC Official, 22/7/2002.

kind. As has been said, social movement unionism lays out a fundamental requirement in the shape of a focus on lower levels of socio-political action, rather than a simple focus on the peak European levels. A shift towards a more multi-level approach both in terms of institutional change and changes in attitudes would also begin to address the problems of the ETUC appearing to be divorced from national unions as was discussed in the previous chapter, as co-ordination and co-operation begins to filter downwards through increased co-operation and linkages to all aspects of the labour movement. It seems that only by such a policy could popular recognition and support be afforded the ETUC, factors critical if it is to be taken seriously by central bodies at the European level of decision making.

In recent years the ETUC appears to have recognised that in the face of supranational pressures, workers need protection afforded not merely by tentative politically led negotiations in Europe, but rather through the development of a true European labour movement[45]. Yet there appears a hesitancy to move beyond an institutionalised, centralist approach that is at odds with the fluidity demanded by new social movement unionism. Rather than focus attention on bringing together

---

45. Interview with ETUC Official, 22/7/2002.

disparate elements of the European labour movement through networking and ground level action, there is instead a desire to attain true, central "European collective Bargaining" (Hoffman, 2000, p640), essentially attempting to stretch existing institutional structures and concepts to fit the modern Europe.

Such a perspective risks failure and indeed irrelevancy, as at present there appears no suitable combination of structure and practice in position for such blanket organisation in Europe. Whilst those within the ETUC may be in favour of shifting labour movement operations towards a centralised European level, corresponding employer will is not present. UNICE has "neither the interest nor the mandate to bargain" (Turner, 1996, p335), stemming from its position as a confederation of private sector employers associations whose primary concern, in direct contrast to that of the ETUC, is to prevent any binding legislation that may hamper capital's manoeuvring position with respect to labour. Thus the UNICE does not possess any actual "mandate from its diverse membership to engage in collective bargaining" (Turner, 1996, p335), meaning the ETUC is in essence attempting to Europeanise collective bargaining without anyone to bargain with.

In 1993 the European Employers' Network (EEN) was

created, though this has been described as a toothless organisation, serving "purely for informal exchange of information and communication ...and is not a body of formal decision making" (Keller and Bansbach, 2001, p427). Thus, with employers having shown "no sign of any willingness to engage in European-level bargaining" (Le Queux and Fajertag, 2001, p130), and a lack of structure in place even if they did, the ETUC could be strengthening its position as a "social partner without a suitor" (Turner, 1996, p335). This situation explicitly highlights the problematic that the ETUC has been built from the top down with little regard for corresponding opponents or popular support, meaning it is essentially a "structure before action" (Dolvik, 1997, pp15). Had support and demand for the ETUC grown from workers and unions, pressure may have come to bear to force other organisations to take it seriously, yet this is opposite to the actual path that has been pursued.

The very composition of the ETUC also seems to hamper moves towards a European level social movement unionism. Composed of national congresses rather than individual unions, the ETUC faces a situation where major members (the British TUC and the German DGB) cannot negotiate directly at their respective national levels (Lecher, 1991, p461). Yet these organisations have close linkages to workers at the national level, through unions that are direct members of the congress and are themselves responsible for ground level organisation and action. In turn these national congresses have legitimate political and economic negotiating partners in the form of national governments and business organisations who are able to enter into binding discussions.

The same cannot be said of the ETUC that is unable to supplement weaknesses through other direct linkages to workers or unions, or through effective mandates to negotiate with willing opponents. Instead the composition of the ETUC risks severely limiting the legitimacy of the ETUC in the eyes of not only capital and political institutions, but the very workers who it is there to defend. For with major members that cannot transfer direct legitimacy or mandate from workers on the ground, the ETUC is in tum unable to claim true legitimacy or even a true mandate for action on behalf of European workers.

Rather than attempting to become a true regional level labour confederation responsible for high level negotiations alone, were the ETUC to pursue a policy influenced by social movement unionism it would radically shift its focus through changes in attitude and institutional practices more open to dealing with social movements, promoting co-operation amongst European labour organisations and engendering popular support for a European labour project. In this conception a "bottom-up" approach (Martin and Ross, 1999, p338) to the protection of workers would be just as important, rather than a heavy reliance on attempts to coalesce "affiliates at both confederal and sectoral levels that have been reluctant and have lacked capacity" (Dolvik, 1997, p21) to shift powers and operations to the European level.

Yet it appears that true moves to transform the ETUC in to a social movement institution have been rejected in favour of 'safer' and more traditional forms of organising. One of these alternatives is a shift of focus towards "a policy of coordinated bargaining in which the EIFs have the prime responsibility" (Waddington, 2001, p460). In rejecting this there is a complete disregard for arguments that traditional forms of operating for the labour movement are ill suited to the modern global political economy, as figures high in the movement simply try another sort of institutionalized action.

A Sectoral Level European Labour Movement?

A sectoral level approach to the Europeanisation of the

labour movement led by EIFs could appear as more palatable to figures at all levels than a wholesale shift to a central level, as "in many European countries the sectoral level is still most important...most European trade unions concur that Europe-wide co- ordination should also have a sectoral focus" (Gollbach and Schulten, 2000, p162). Fourteen EIFs operate within Europe and are affiliated as members of the ETUC. The ETUC expressed resignation that attempts to build a centralised system of peak level bargaining within Europe has been ill fated, formally agreeing in 1999 that EIFs should "take primary responsibility for co-ordinated collective bargaining at European level" (Le Queux and Fajertag, 2001, p 117). Being a step closer to unions and their members through their direct linkages, the EIFs appear to be in a relatively strong position to fight for worker's interests across Europe as their structures "allow relatively straight forward combinations of unions to pursue interests of common concern" (Waddington, 2000, p326). It appears that there is a growing shift in attitude within the ETUC that sees such linkages to workers as an important strength essential for any organisation that wishes to provide dynamic leadership above the national level. And in turn a recognition that a development of the role of EIFs could serve to bring workers closer to the processes at the European level.

To bring sectoral level organisations to the fore appears to represent a capitulation on behalf of the ETUC, with the struggle for support and influence being seen as beyond its capabilities in its present form. But again this highlights an unwillingness to substantially change the processes and structures within the ETUC, with simply a shifting of responsibility for the same procedural goals being made. One positive element of a shift towards sectoral level bargaining is that support from the national level is more likely as unions need not fear that their powers are being moved to a divorced power centre[46]. Yet attitudes of elements other than trade unions at the national level hamper moves towards a sectoral level labour movement. National congresses that compose the ETUC fear that a strengthening of the EIFs position would equate to a weakening of their own (Hyman, 2001). This is a mirroring of the attitudes presented by their member unions at the national level who are fearful of change in case existing power is lost, and serves to highlight important tensions that flow through all levels of the European labour movement, as different elements jostle for positions of power at the European level. National congresses

---

46. Interview with TUC Official, 27/6/2002.

appear keen to keep power concentrated at the more institutionalised level that the ETUC represents, possibly in a bid to increase their relative power positions "vis-a-vis affiliated unions" (Waddington, 2000, p326), but doing so shows a lack of commitment to the European ideal.

Despite the reservations of some within the labour movement, there are benefits to be had from a sectoral focused dimension of European labour politics. Within this model of clearer lines of communication and decision making from the ground level worker up to the sectoral level EIF, there is potential for workers to become more actively involved in the Europeanisation of the labour movement. This is in the spirit of conditions argued for by social movement unionism, and because of the ties between the EIFs and the ETUC, this could also lead to a transferring of legitimacy and support towards the ETUC in an organic and natural manner. This would occur as the European dimension of the labour movement is defined for the first time by linkages that have workers in a central position.

Members of national unions would have a vested interest in developments at the European level as they are directly involved through a series of linkages between worker and union, union and EIF, and EIF and ETUC. It is only human nature that workers would then be in a position to take interest in developments at the European level as the line of impact that they have on their everyday lives is made clear for all to see. This interest would combine with the fact that as workers vote on developments within national unions that in turn have input into the ElFs that are linked to the ETUC, to mean that the European level labour movement would have legitimacy and a mandate. As a co-ordination network and information net is created (Gobin, 1994, p244) through the ETUC- EIF structure, there is the added potential that social movement unionism could become an important model for organisation. This would occur as human issues are transferred from bottom-up to provide an impetus for lasting changes in structures and practice as those at the highest levels are made more aware of the situations facing workers and the impacts that their decisions have on them.

Such optimistic visions of progress appear unlikely however, because the issue of EIFs becoming bargaining bodies raises conflict between national unions and confederations. As has been stated, national confederations appear uneasy that they may lose power and influence that has already been eroded in the wake of pressures if powers were to be invested in EIFs (Le Queux and Fajertag, 2001). Juxtaposed to this position is that of national unions who often feel they "are divorced from the ETUC and what happens at the European level"47 . These unions are on the whole much more in favour of having an increased role for EIFs as they effectively control these organisations due to direct linkages and processes of policy formulation (Martin and Ross, 1999, p341). In this sense EIFs represent a more 'bottom up' approach to developing a European labour movement, yet still in an institutionalised formation familiar to the labour movement, rather than a completely fluid movement akin to social movements that have been rejected as partners by unions. They may be argued to be essentially international trade unions, able to fight for worker's rights across national borders, but in doing so they also still harbour the same problems as their national counterparts, such as a lack of urgent militancy and solid, often inflexible working structures.

Indeed, much of the ElF's strengths are merely apparent in comparison with the marginalised ETUC, and not other societal groupings. For whilst it is possible to argue that EIFs share a collective capacity for disruption and organisation similar to national unions, it must be remembered that the loss of power suffered by those national unions who compose EIFs

---

47. Interview with GMB Official, 27/5/2002.

is precisely why an internationalisation of the labour movement is argued for. So EIFs appear more powerful than the weak ETUC, yet their power only comes from weakened national organisations in need of renewal. Despite this it appears at present that EIFs are "the only part of the existing European trade union structure through which unions might be willing to organise cross border co-ordination of bargaining" (Martin and Ross, 1999, p341). But again, recognising the arguments presented in discussions of social movement unionism leads us to see that simply shifting operations up to this sectoral level without any substantive reforms of practice or structure is to simply shuffle existing problems around. There is at present no real groundswell of support for even this less centralised European level labour movement, and as was the case with the centralised ETUC, there is again an "absence of employers' organisations prepared to enter into bargaining arrangements" (Waddington, 2000, p326).

The employers' associations that exist are mainly in "narrowly defined sub- sectors, and often they are generally business rather than specific employers' associations" (Keller and Bansbach, 2001, p427). This situation can be argued to be a result of industry's desire to push dialogue and structures not upwards to a supranational level that may aid labour in the modern world, but instead to "drive collective bargaining down to the company level" (Martin, 1999, p22) where control over work is easier to gain and retain. It appears then that the conditions necessary for an issue driven, multi-level form of action are yet to be met in the EU. And as will be discussed later in this chapter, a combination of factors repeatedly present major stumbling blocks to any meaningful developments at the European level, other than a continual reliance on forms of institutional structures that are individually inadequate to meet the demands they face.

Corporate Level Industrial Relations?

European Works Councils (EWCs) are yet another level of the Europeanisation of the labour movement, and can be seen as an attempt to get "some worker representation at the company level that capital is so determined to operate at"[48]. However these councils embody many of the problems that run throughout the European level of industrial relations. Central to the reasoning behind these problems is that EWCs do not come from coherent

48. Interview with TUC Official, 27/6/2002.

agreements between capital and labour, but have rather been imposed from above by political institutions following a failed process of legislation (Lecher and Rub, 1999). The European Commission called upon the ETUC and UNICE to agree upon a process for worker's rights to information and consultation, but "UNICE did not receive a negotiating mandate and refused to hold talks" (Waddington and Hoffman, 2000, p644). As such the councils were imposed upon the societal actors from above in an artificial manner that lead to a lack of legitimacy and support.

Despite the description of EWCs as "a major step towards pan European structures and collective bargaining" (Martin and Ross, 1997, p342) by UNICE, their level of impact upon workers lives is debatable. In an optimistic reading EWCs may be seen as a form of "catalyst in the Europeanisation of industrial relations" (Waddington and Hoffman, 2000, p647). Yet from a pessimistic perspective they provide legitimisation for poor work standards and practices across the region of Europe as their very presence within a workplace may allow a veneer of social co-operation and compliance to appear. These councils operate only with mandates to provide networks for information exchange for workers within specific workplaces (Martin and Ross, p342), so it seems unlikely that they will provide a radical Europeanisation of the labour movement in terms of institutional change. Instead it appears that if EWCs are to have a major impact on workers' lives, they will provide a framework within which co-operation and communication may lead to wider changes in attitudes and then practice (Lecher et al, 1999, p73).

As EWCs spread around Europe it is argued that if supported effectively by the labour movement as a whole, they "may provide a basis for a broadening transnational exchange between management and labour as well as between worker's representatives from below" (Dolvik, 1997, p 11). Such a framework of co-ordination could mirror the information networks that are an integral part of the new forms of organising as pointed to by social movement unionism. In a sense EWCs could allow the labour movement to 'steal a march' on its capital counterpart if dynamic and fluid policies are enacted to "subvert information flows within companies in order to develop transnational networks that undermined the operation of management" (Taylor and Mathers, 2002, p99). Yet as will be argued, despite these conditions being set out by social movement unionist theory, the observable situation is somewhat different.

Some of the main supporting arguments for EWCs are somewhat negative in their tone, arguing that those within the labour movement who are sceptical of the merits of the internationalisation of the labour movement, may be more willing to accept EWCs as a 'soft option'[49]. Whilst the creation of information networks by "linking representatives in different EWCs with one another as well as those in other companies" (Martin and Ross, 1999, p344) may be a positive step, it is not the militant and wide reaching transformation of the labour movement that some would argue for. As such there are some within the labour movement who have been moved to describe this company level framework as "not enough" and as being simple "company institutions[50] highlighting a discontent with piecemeal developments that echoes scepticism with more substantive moves.

The lack of obvious enthusiasm from some within the labour movement regarding the development of EWCs presents dual points for debate. First is a possibility that those within the labour movement view any development that has even the potential to take any powers or tasks away from national trade unions as threatening. Yet this view appears to ignore the argument inherent in social movement unionism that existing structures in the labour movement are already weakened and that internationalisation in various fashions is an element of the policy

---

49. Interview with WCL Official, 24/7/2002
50. Interview with GMB Official, 27/5/2002.

for renewal.

The second cause for concern is the criticism that EWCs may promise much but are lacking in substance. Despite being mandatory in all companies employing more than 1000 workers, EWCs still cover little more than 10% of the total workforce in Europe (Martin, 1999, p23), meaning that they are of little importance to many workers. Whilst even if they spread to cover a much larger proportion of European workers and workplaces, they are limited by legislation that argues they are to be "mere forums for information exchange" (Martin, 1999, p23). It will prove difficult for the labour movement to build upon the potential opening given by EWCs[51] bearing in mind the inevitable opposition that employers would bring to bear and the lack of commitment within the labour movement shown towards a wide ranging programme of reform at all levels of the movement.

Even if EWCs do spread to cover every part of Europe, there is the possibility that MNCs may attempt to use them for their own purposes, namely the instillation of "corporate-specific employment regimes cutting across labour markets" (Le Queux and Fajertag, 2001, p120). Indeed there are countries such as Germany who argued against EWCs, as they appeared in such

---

51. Interview with ETUC Official, 2217/2002.

weak form that they weakened the industrial relations framework provided by their domestic works councils. With just as much potential to provide "transnational micro-corporatism" (Le Queux and Fajertag, 2001, p120) as a framework for the development of a European social movement unionism, EWCs show tensions and contradictions that require strong action on behalf of the labour movement.

Analysing attitudes and practices across Europe suggests that fears EWCs "could undermine national union structures without contributing anything to the construction of European structures to replace them" (Martin, 1999, p23) are over dramatic. It would take a reversal of trajectory and opinion if a situation where "works councils may give employees the feeling that unions are not necessary any more" (Blaschke, 2000, p230) is to develop.

This research builds upon arguments that workers need protection provided by a co-ordinated, dynamic, issue led movement that spans national borders, not merely facilities to exchange information and ideas between workplaces. Yet whilst this limitation to information exchange limits EWCs potential, it also means that they provide a viable starting point for the development of a social movement unionism based on co-operation and co-ordination. Such "cross-border collaboration"

(Waddington, 2000, p327) is argued to be vital for the future, yet at present the ETUC is often outside developments, meaning there is at times a lack of leadership or co-ordination as to what policy of internationalisation is to be taken.

The building of Interregional Trade Union Councils (ITUCs) that allow for cross border communication and collaboration on various issues (Waddington, 2000, p327) has largely been due to proactive national unions, highlighting the ad-hoc nature of many successful developments as prescribed frameworks from above have been deemed as failures. The GMB in Britain has been keen to develop such inter union linkages precisely due to the distance felt between themselves and prevailing European level structures[52], showing that not all attitudes are in need of change.

It was as early as 1997 that this union signed a joint membership agreement with the German chemical union IG Chernie-Papier- Kerarnik, prompting the question of whether there were "European super unions on the horizon?" (EFILWC, 1997). That unions find themselves in a position where the ETUC, EIFs and EWCs exist, yet they still prefer to develop their own European labour movement shows on the one hand the

---

52. Interview with GMB Official, 27/5/2002.

irrelevant nature that current structures take, and on the other the hope that there is a will for a redrawing of the contemporary labour movement (Gollbach and Schulten, 2000).

A Rejection of Social Movement Unionism at the European Level?

Despite the existence of three elements of a potential framework for a European labour movement, several key stumbling blocks to the internationalisation of the movement as inherent in social movement unionism have been identified. These relate to the necessary conditions for Europeanisation as outlined earlier in this chapter, inspired as they are by the social movement unionism that informs this research. First is the argument that the lack of a significant European capital organisation has hampered moves to internationalise the labour movement at both the central and sectoral levels (Waddington, 2000, p326).

Concerns that European capital "doesn't really care what labour organisations develop as they don't feel any pressing need to get involved"[53] is symptomatic of a malaise regarding the Europeanisation of the labour movement. Secondly, an over reliance on political institutions and their pro labour leanings

---

53. Interview with ETUC Official, 22/7/2002.

(Hyman, 2001) has led to a situation whereby the European labour movement can be perceived as less a social movement and more a political tool. This intertwines with perhaps the largest stumbling block to a true European labour movement, namely the lack of popular support from the very workers around Europe who are to be protected. This has occurred as the process of internationalising the labour movement across Europe has been promoted from the top-down, rather than through an organic process of engendering support by highlighting key issues and the importance of the European level for workers and unions alike.

Instead of "trying to arouse interest in European matters" (Goetschy, 1996, p262) through dynamic campaigns of action or organisation, the ETUC has followed a path aimed at political influence that is divorced from the experience of most workers. This has resulted in a situation whereby the ETUC is essentially a "structure before action" (Turner, 1996, p325), largely irrelevant not only for workers but indeed for many national unions who appear wary of transferring any of their already weakened powers to a level apparently lacking effectiveness. Those who argue that popular support and solidarity may not be prerequisites for the Europeanisation of the labour movement, relying instead on social spill over theory (Hyman, 2001, p290) miss the point.

A European dimension to the labour movement is a social framework, it is an element of the globalising of civil society and due to its very societal and human nature cannot be imposed in any way, but must rather be developed organically. Changes to existing institutional structures and practices are only part of a larger shift needed to lead to an encompassing change across the European labour movement, as changes in attitudes from all figures and organisations are just as necessary. As was argued in the previous chapter, for effective change to occur, there must be an adequate combination of both these elements, yet at present both sides to the process are fractured at best.

A set of "networks of contacts and new structures" (Turner, 1996, p329) that uses the existing institutional frameworks of the ETUC, could conceivably interact with sectoral level EIFs and company level EWCs to provide a multi-level framework within which the Europeanisation of labour could take place. The construction of a wide ranging dialogue between the ETUC and other social movements has the potential to address a situation pointed to in the previous chapter whereby national figures feel divorced from the highest European levels, by bringing the organisation into a clearer focus for those at the ground level, and this in turn could form a part of a process to change attitudes within the labour movement.

There are a wide variety of NGOs and other social movements operating in Europe that are in a position to interact with the ETUC and other European level organisations (Hyman, 2001, p292), and an interaction with such organisations would fulfil certain elements of social movement unionism discussed in this research such as a need to learn and use more dynamic forms of operating. By working closely with social movements the ETUC would be able to learn the importance of forms of organisation and action that are less solid than the institutional form currently adopted, meaning they are able to operate as an effective societal actor outside the corridors of power at the highest level. Simultaneously, such a policy of dynamic action would serve to make the European level of the labour movement more visible and relevant as an element of civil society, a move that could engender popular support currently missing (Gill and Krieger, 2000).

Within organisations such as the ETUC there have been skeptical attitudes towards either the real need to change practices or processes, or indeed towards the merits of other social movements. There are some who argue that "NGOs must grow up and look beyond their simple parameters"[54] before

---

54. Interview with ETUC Official, 22/7/2002.

they could be brought into the processes at work at the European level. This seems to mirror a belief prevalent at the national level of the labour movement that other social movements are somehow less worthwhile than trade unions that are seen as the "genuine social movements"[55]. It also portrays a certain assumption that these movements will be 'brought into' something that the trade unions are currently commanding, when in reality it appears that labour organisations are on the periphery of a civil society containing other social movements. Rather than looking towards other social movements for inspiration and assistance (Munck, 1998), the ETUC as peak European labour body seems keener to argue the labour movement will somehow naturally take on board social issues that are not initially part of the 'worker-focused' remit[56].

There is a rejection of new strategies and instead a fear that to co-operate with other movements or redevelop existing structures would lead to "unions be[ing] lumped in with women's groups in an amalgam that will not get anything done"[57]. Attitudes that NGOs are not to be trusted as "power

---

55. Interview with ETUC Official, 22/7/2002.
56. Interview with ETUC Official, 22/7/2002.
57. Interview with ETUI Researcher, 23/7/2002.

is often from top down in NGOs and they aren't as democratic as the ETUC"[58] also seem to show that at the European level as at the national level, there is a fear that to change the prevailing structures and practices of the labour movement will be to reject the essence of being a labour movement. Yet this position is shortsighted and ignores the fact that the movement in its current form is still marginalised, and at the regional level lacks amongst other things fundamental ground level support (Gobin, 1994).

A prevailing attitude that the ETUC and its member confederations have sole "representative capacity for society in Europe"[59] seems to be fostering a myopic arrogance that sees no real challenge to its position. Even with the development of EIFs and EWCs, those within the ETUC still see themselves as the ultimate heads of a European labour movement, yet this again ignores the weak position their organisation finds itself in following the challenges presented by globalisation and the problems surrounding the European level of the labour movement as discussed here.

---

58. Interview with ETUC Official, 22/7/2002.
59. Interview with ETUC Official, 22/7/2002.

Conclusion: A Multi-Layered European Social Movement Unionism?

It is imperative that if the trade unions are to become revitalised and find a position from where they can better react to contemporary pressures, they must look beyond their national boundaries (Waterman, 1998). This chapter has analysed the three main levels in which such internationalisation has been attempted, namely the company level, the sectoral level and a centralised European level.

It has been argued that the key stumbling blocks in the path to successful internationalisation of the labour movement lie with national actor's reluctance to commit to actions that they feel may threaten their constituency, the lack of an effective or viable employer body to negotiate with, a historical reliance on political will for progress and a resultant lack of mass popular support amongst civil society for the ETUC.

All of these stumbling blocks have been amplified by an apparent rejection of the most fundamental tenants of social movement unionism at the European level, namely increased linkages with other social movements and resultant fundamental changes in both structures and practice that would complement structural frameworks for Europeanisation presented by EIFs,

EWCs and the ETUC.

Having analysed the efficacy of each of the three levels of the European labour movement, it appears that progress towards institutional change within existing frameworks, and attitudinal change with regards to organisations and objectives, must occur at all three levels, or at least more than one if the labour movement is to successfully regionalise. A viable vision of the future may include the ETUC as a principal organising body, with EIFs and EWCs operating beneath in differing yet intertwining roles. Such a strategy recognises and encompasses processes and structures from all interconnected levels of action in the global era, from the local to the transnational.

The ETUC currently argues that the best that can be hoped for in the future is "federalism and not centralization"[60] and in doing so misses the potential that exists for a truly decentralised, network based European social movement unionism. Such a notion of the Europeanisation of the labour movement recognises that the national level is still a critical battleground within which battles must be fought and support won (Dolvik, 1997, p11), whilst also recognising that inspiration, support and co- ordination is required from above the national

---

60. Interview with ETUC Official, 22/7/2002.

level if transnational capital and neo-liberalism are to be countered.

If the actors at the higher European levels were able to reassure national trade unions that they do not intend to pursue a policy of development that would wrestle powers away from the national to the European level, then unions may be more willing to lend their support and influence[61] (Hoffman and Hoffman, 2001). A move away from the institutional and often aloof nature that the ETUC in particular operates would start movement along such a path.

A development of a social movement unionist strategy by the ETUC that facilitates successful interaction across the region, could herald a "dual system in which the hard core of industrial relations persists at the national level, though increasingly embedded in European frameworks for transnational co-ordination" (Dolvik, 1997, p12). By linking to other social movements it seems conceivable that the ETUC could become a central element of a meaningful social coalition for European workers, thus increasing its support, whilst also learning new practices that would allow for its development into a prime site for co-ordination between other actors such as

---

61. Interview with GMB Official, 27/5/2002.

unions and EIFs. With the ETUC as a hub for the Europeanised labour movement, sectoral level EIFs would play a critical role in the real world implementation and co-ordination of region wide strategies and information exchange.

This resonates with arguments that "EIFs seem to be the only cross-border union structures so far available with some prospect of serving as a mechanism" (Martin, 1999, p23) for co-ordinating the European labour movement. The emergent dynamic and relevant European social movement unionism embedded within European civil society could engender support at the national level for such moves, thus sparking a rejuvenation of the labour movement, with EWCs being used as vehicles for exchanges of information and experiences (Lecher and Rub, 1999, p23), that if neglected could be developed along the lines perceived by capital (Lecher and Rub, 1999, p8).

For the above to take place, the substantial stumbling blocks would have to be recognised and challenged, but in doing so the "internationalisation" (Moody, 1997) pointed to by social movement unionism could be attained. Workers would be represented by organisations that have increased capacity for action due to the cross-border networks that would also provide increased information, expertise and understanding of contemporary issues in the wider world. Within the multi-level

European labour movement national unions would remain a key constituent being responsible for much action and policy implementation. Therefore trade unionists would not have to unnecessarily surrender powers to higher level organisations (Waddington and Hoffman, 2000, p327) without seeing any gains. Instead they would become part of a larger entity within which national borders are but a small piece of the vision and strategy.

Bearing in mind the scepticism shown both at the European and British level towards social movements within civil society, it is important to analyse whether the labour movement is actually compatible with them. For if the arguments promoted in this and previous chapters are to be followed successfully, it is important that the reality of negative arguments are understood. With this in mind the next chapter will analyse the issues surrounding civil society and social movements at the global level of analysis, paying particular attention to the structure and organisations that exist that could point to the potential for the labour movement to successfully interact with other social movements, and develop along social movement unionist lines.

5. GLOBAL FRAMEWORKS FOR SOCIAL MOVEMENT UNIONISM

Introduction

The previous chapter analysed the labour related frameworks and organisations that exist at the European level, and the extent to which they have facilitated a shifting upwards of practices from the national to the regional level. It was argued that the effective Europeanisation of the labour movement was being hampered in a variety of ways. Deficiencies in institutional and structural practices that whilst important for the Europeanisation of the labour movement, are not sufficient conditions for the process if in isolation.

It was argued that there was a reluctance on the part of certain members of the labour movement to pursue key themes of social movement unionism, a continued rejection of increased linkages to other social movements, and a narrow perspective on what is in the best interests of the labour movement. These combined with the lack of comparable business organisations, an over-reliance on political institutions, and a lack of popular support to hamper any shift towards a European social movement union model being developed.

This chapter continues the exploration of conditions for social movement unionism by shifting the focus upward to the global level. Having provided analysis of the key global labour organisations and the fractured relationship that exists between them, it will be shown to what extent those operating at this level are committed to social movement unionism. This is an important question as policies and practices emanating from this level have the potential to shape and inform those at the national and regional levels, just as the creation of coherent practices and processes at the lower levels has the potential to impact upon this global dimension. Again it will be shown that structural, institutional and attitudinal issues hinder progress towards social movement unionism at this level, as consensus between key organisations is scarce, whilst the same institutional traditionalism exists as was seen at the national and European levels.

When analysis is centred on the global dimension of the labour movement and the political economy in which it operates, the importance of the non-standard/informal economy that was first mentioned in chapter three also becomes clear. Labour related issues that may appear as somewhat removed from tangible experience at the national or regional level, become more central to our understanding of the international political economy of labour. With this in mind the analysis moves to the informal economy, and the group of organisations that have grown to represent workers all too often seen as somehow external to the world of work as envisaged in national/regional conceptions.

It will be argued that the workers within this element of the global political economy are not only a social grouping in need of support and protection, but that they also provide a large potential new constituency that could empower trade unions. Despite this the global level of the labour movement shows little real urgency in addressing their issues, in no small way due to a rejection of social movement unionism. Of great importance for this research is the fact that organisations representing workers in this economy have looked beyond traditional organisations and frameworks towards a form of social movement unionism.

Organisations such as Self-Employed Women's Association (SEWA) (set up in 1972 to protect women working in the informal sector) and Women in Informal Employment Globalizing and Organizing (WIEGO) could provide a working example of social movement unionism, and in doing so are essentially a test for the effectiveness of this ethos rejected by the traditional labour movement. This model of organisation is seen to be the best practice for trade unions in the global age, if they are indeed close to the model of social movement unionism detailed in this thesis. Whilst the labour movement in its traditional form may not be in a position to directly and immediately transfer all the practices and structures held by organisations such as WIEGO, the recurring argument that there is a need for changes in both attitudes, structures and practices presents the process in which the 'new' model could be transferred through a progressive shift rather than immediate revolution.

The final section will move to point to World Social Forums (WSFs) as an opportunity for the labour movement to come into contact with other elements of civil society in a fashion that may in the future ease any progressive shift towards new forms of organisation. In a sense these forums will be argued to be instrumental in moves towards developing new fashions of operating and organising through a reaching "out to other social movements" (O'Brien, 2000b, p515) that will allow the traditional labour movement to develop in similar fashions to the new 'self organising' groups discussed.

The Global Dimension of the Labour Movement

Of prime importance for this research are the central labour organisations that extend beyond the state and regional levels to form what is termed here the global dimension of the labour movement. Whilst it may be true to argue that this level is not as coherent or well developed as the traditional level of the nation state, there are nonetheless a series of linkages, organisations, institutions and movements that interconnect to provide at least a developing global dimension.

Indeed these may be seen as an important element of the global civil society discussed in chapter three, mirroring necessarily the shifting upwards of power and influence to the global level (Cox, 1983). Whilst the outcomes of many initiatives at this level may appear to be of little consequence for workers in less developed areas of the world[62] , and they are necessarily based in a particular nation, organisations are nonetheless built upon global ethics and ideals. And if a series of organisations, linkages and programmes directed at the global level of action and co-ordination of the labour movement do not imply a global dimension, it is unclear what will.

---

62. Interview with IGTLWF Official, 7/8/2002.

At this global level of the labour movement we can observe clearly developed institutions that present frameworks for organising and action. These include the International Confederation of Trade Unions (ITUC), International Labour Organisation (ILO) and a host of International Trade Secretariats (ITSs).

Today then we have the ITUC, representing over 180 million workers through 380 affiliated federations. On the face of it the labour movement has a centralised framework for organisation and action. The ITUC was created in 2006 through the merger of the International Confederation of Free Trade Unions (ICFTU) and World Confederation of Labour (WCL). But it represents the amalgamation of two wildly divergent organisations, with different historic priorities and a lingering mistrust of one another.

Traditionally, the most important of these organisations was seen as the ICFTU that comprised "independent and democratic trade unions from around the world, representing 127 million people from 136 countries" (O'Brien, 2000c, p542). Focus was often centered on this organisation to the detriment of the less dominant WCL that, despite disdain shown by the ICFTU with its claim the WCL was merely a "relatively small organisation based on Christian social principles" (ICFTU, 200

I), still claimed to represent 23.7million workers world-wide (as of 1996).

Conflict and fracturing long appeared to hamper cohesive action at the global level of the labour movement, stemming from ideological divisions that were highly visible during the cold war (O'Brien, 2000c, p536). The ICFTU was founded out of conflict within the labour movement, "to battle communist unions" (O'Brien, 2000c, p536) that were prevalent around the world. As such it became primarily the 'western' global union, leaving its major counterpart the WCL to organise and protect workers from the East and South.

The fact that fracturing between differing worldviews formed the basis of the ICFTU means that negativity defined the 'inside' of the organisation, with its practices and structures developing as a response to external threats rather than the explicit needs of all workers. The fracturing between the two organisations continued for many years, with primary research indicating attitudes within the ICFTU and WCL differed just as much as policies regarding territorial boundaries and priorities for action[63]. A pessimistic perspective from the interview material concludes that the ICFTU in particular developed a

---

63. Interview with WCL Official, 24/7/2002.

siege mentality, affecting its attitudes towards other elements of the labour movement and civil society at large that are outside the boundaries of the organisation.

The differing dimensions and strengths of the two organisations led to a divergence of organisation and action with regards to efforts in the political economy shaped by globalisation pressures discussed in chapter three. The ICFTU tended towards more visible, high level operations than the marginalised WCL that was forced into more ground level initiatives in the mould of social movement unionism, as it lacked the funds, staff and influence of the ICFTU.

In a sense the ICFTU represented 'old', more traditional form of labour movement that is reliant on political avenues and institutionalised practices, whilst the WCL pursued (often not through choice), a form of social movement unionism that relied on more low cost, dynamic and ground level forms of operation. The WCL in this sense represented a halfway house between traditional institutional trade unionism and social movement unionism, with ground level initiatives and social co-operation occurring within a globalised hierarchy and structure.

There was scepticism within both organisations regarding amalgamation or to a certain extent even deep cooperation. ICFTU officials did want to link both organisations to build numbers and reduce costs but simply did not believe in the social movement perspective of the WCL which was seen as "unrealistic as unions are the only ones elected to represent"[64] people. The WCL opposed any amalgamation of the global labour movement, because it was "dangerous to infer rashly the expediency of a single trade union structure as the international level" (WCL, 2001, p34), as worker's interests are best served with a pluralism and sensitivity that exists within the present multi-organisational structure. The fear was that were the WCL and ICFTU to merge, the social values that remain very focused on gaining benefits for workers at the ground level would be lost in the wake of the much more global multilateralist perspective of the ICFTU.

Fast forward to the present day and the ICFTU is *the* global labour federation[65], created in a bid to cut costs, increase efficiencies and create some sort of critical mass in place instead of sector division. It covers all continents and it can be argued, is too

---

64. Interview with ICFTU Official, 24/7/2002.

65. See Windmuller, J. P. Pursey, S. K. and Baker, J. (2014) The International Trade Union Movement in Blanpain, R. eds. (2014) Comparative Labour Law and Industrial Relations in Industrialized Market Economies, pp. 75–100for excellent overview of the ITUC, its formation, organisation and activities.

big to focus on the detailed issues that most visibly change lives. The fact that the organisation spans ideological boundaries with "many, perhaps most, of the affiliates of the ICFTU...from socialist or social democratic traditions and most, but not all of the WCL affiliates were originally inspired by Christian values." (Windmuller et al. 20114, p75) can be argued to inhibit its focus. To avoid fracturing the ITUC's values are therefore necessarily broad including, for example, defence of human rights, or opposition to totalitarianism.

It appears that any focus on social movement unionism that might have been held by the WCL has been eroded through partnership. The focus of the ITUC is more akin to the traditional ICFTU – lobbying national governments using member federations, and linking to international bodies such as the OECD's TUAC (Trade Union Advisory Committee). This institutional focus carries risks – not least that non-labour organisations can become "strategy on the part of the dominant power gradually to co-opt elements of opposition forces" (Cox, 1999, p16).

Here the very societal actors that wish to challenge the status quo are in the end "authorising and legitimating the practices of the formal institutions of global governance" (Amoore and Langley, 2004, p97). This occurred in the 1990s when the

ICFTU invested huge resource and effort into labour standards being attached to WTO trade agreements (Wilkinson and Hughes, 2000). Despite optimism from inside the ICFTU, this was not straightforward, and the WTO shifted the debate towards the development of "ILO-regulated" (Wilkinson and Hughes, 2000, p262) standards.

Another aspect of the ITUC's work appears to echo the more ground-level WCL of the past - reinforcing unionism where unions are weak, mainly through training union officers (Windmuller et al. 20114, p82). This type of work can be seen to build on a historic WCL commitment to tapping human agency to drive change. Indeed, the WCL was to an extent defined by historic "contacts...with a whole range of NGOs like human rights watch" (WCL, 2001, p19) and the belief that co-operation with social movements can give "youth and freshness to the union movement"[66]. But this human element of the ITUC's agenda lacks funding and visibility when compared to other more structure of institution-focused work. There is little to suggest that much is being done to "reach out to other social movements" (O'Brien, 2000b, p515), perhaps reflecting the old ICFTU sceptisim surrounding new ways of working, and social movements

---

66. Interview with WCL Official, 24/7/2002.

themselves.

As was once argued by a senior ICFTU leader - NGOs and the like "do not need to stay in the real world ...they ask for unrealistic things"[67]. This highlights the extent to which many within the global and indeed national and regional labour movements, see any form of politics outside traditional structures as somehow invalid. This in turn signposts a rejection of social movement unionism that was in the ITUC from day one due to the ICFTU's position, with it being argued long ago that "the lack of democracy in NGOs etc means the union- NGO relationship can only really be for single issues, afterwards we have to say goodbye"[68]. So for the ICFTU and now ITUC, the focus is often on 'safe' issues and partners, rather than fluidity or dynamism.

In a sense therefore we see an implicit, and long term rejection of social movement unionism by first the ICFI'U and now ITUC. This is especially damaging to workers when global issues are brought into focus. Perhaps most important of these issues, bearing in mind the challenges of globalised production and technology discussed in chapter three, is the increasing prevalence of the informal economy in the modern global political economy.

---

67. Interview with ICFTU Official, 24/7/2002.
68. Interview with ICFTU Official, 24/7/2002.

The key issues at stake will now be analysed, in order that the importance of a coherent, socially focused response from the organisations is shown.

The Informal Economy in the Global Focus

Whilst at the national and European levels of the labour movement more traditional forms of work are most observable, a shift in focus upwards brings the informal economy explicitly into view due to its very global nature. In order to address the issues faced by workers in this economy, and incorporate them into the global labour community, a change of policy and practice is necessary on behalf of the labour movement as a whole, something that would be afforded by a more united stance that pursues dynamic practices less reliant on formal institutions. This is because the informal economy by its very nature often exists outside the remit of the traditional socio-political framework, so to rely on traditional institutions and methods seems somewhat doomed to failure. An effective way of representing and organising workers in this area of the global political economy would require dynamic and progressive structures and practices that effectively addresses the challenges and opportunities presented by globalisation, in a manner that takes social agency as being central. Any effective adoption of such policies could present a possible model for the future development of the labour movement as a whole.

The informal economy is seen as comprising "a vast range of activities in which workers generally operate in oppressive and unsafe working conditions, with incomes often at or below the poverty line and little or no access to state- provided social protection, training and social services" (ILO, 1999, p3). Despite calls to organise this element of the global political economy, the importance of such a move is "not recognised equally by all sections of the trade union movement" (Gallin, 2001, p1).

Variously, some in the labour movement believe that the informal economy will somehow formalise itself or that it is not as large and important as some believe: perspectives that lead to some involved in the labour movement paying scant attention to the sector[69]. This ignores caveats from those who have acknowledged that unprotected workers operating within the informal economy are a central issue for the global labour movement[70]. Yet for the most part the traditional labour movement operates within the formal socio-political framework

69. Interview with ETUC Official, 22/7/2002.
70. Interview with TUC Official, 27/6/2002.

214

removed from the informal economy. As such it encounters difficulty in addressing or indeed recognising the issues faced outside the formal sector, and the potentials that are held there.

To think of the informal economy is to bring forth images of sweat shops, back street businesses, as well as home and domestic workers that seem detached from most traditional experiences of work. Yet it is difficult to categorise, not least because it operates out of clear view, both below and behind the traditional economy that forms much of the focus for IPE (Bauman, 1998).

The ILO has attempted to define the informal sector by listing some of its main properties including "ease of entry ...labour intensive work, using adaptive technologies ...an irregular and competitive market" (Bullock, 1994, p56). Whilst such a conceptualisation highlights the fluid nature of the informal economy, the most important aspect of this part of the modern global political economy is "the absence of rights and social protection" (WIEGO, 2003d, p3) for those involved. This means that workers within this sector do not have access to the protection that may at the very least be fought for by those working in the more traditional, formal sector.

Yet it is important that the informal sector is not seen as an entirely separate entity from the formal economy, for there exist a set of "linkages and power relationships between the informal economy and formal sector" (WIEGO, 2001, p6) that means a division between the two is an artificial construct. The reality is that forms of work within the informal economy are necessary for the "economic survival" (Edwards and Arango, 1999, p11) of states and companies that form much of the labour movement's focus.

Figures show that work outside the formal sector already accounts for some 80% of all work done in low-income countries, and a still important 15% for countries deemed to have a high income (Gallin, 2001, p533). And the economy grows larger for "when jobs grow scarce, these [informal] activities become the only life buoy for countless families" (WCL, 2001a, p1). The ignorance of this dimension of the global political economy as most of the labour movement rejects the inclusive social movement unionism, means that many workers are cut adrift from potential support and protection.

That the importance of the informal economy is not "recognised equally by all sections of the trade union movement' (WIEGO, 2003d, p1) could be explained by the argument that the informal economy somehow threatens the traditional labour movement, with informal workers appearing to "pose a serious threat to their effectiveness and power" (Rowbotham and Mitter,

1994, p39) as a social and political actor. This could be conceived by officials fearing that the formal work undertaken within their remit is undermined by the informal economy. Such attitudes are defensive, and highlight an unwillingness to adopt policies of change that may undermine perceived positions of power held by labour figures as discussed in previous chapters.

To ignore this informal economy and the workers involved is to ignore a "critical mass in terms of membership and representativity it needs to be a credible social and political force" (WIEGO, 2003d, p4). Yet there is a reluctance to do anything more substantial on behalf of trade unions than artificially extending the "field of activity to include informal sector workers" (Gallin, 2001, p538), in a manner that does not fully incorporating new worker's needs or perspectives.

Such attempts to bring informal workers into the fold are flawed as the experiences and needs of workers across the globe are so divergent from those of the traditional labour movement that any attempt to universalise the movement and it's values simply alienates what are heterogeneous groups of workers (Leacock and Safa, 1986, p264). Rather than wait for institutionalised labour organisation such as the ICFTU to address their situations, workers now find themselves participating in a dynamic and fluid form of organising that could prove the true potential for social movement unionism in the globalised era, whilst simultaneously further threatening the position of more traditional trade unions.

New Forms of Labour Organisations in the Global Focus

Various groups of workers have in recent times been represented by organisations that have side-stepped the process of relying on traditional frameworks and understandings. There are at present a number of interlinked groups that are developing to help organise and protect particularly women and other workers within the informal economy, which the traditional labour movement has yet to adequately address. In doing so they present an expression of social movement unionism, challenging the attitudes and frameworks of the traditional labour movement that has often ignored anything outside the formal and traditional workplace.

Homenet (that supports home-based workers), SEWA, WIEGO and StreetNet (that protects and organises street-based workers), are prominent amongst such groups that have been at the forefront of organising workers in precarious employment around the world. These organisations have developed in a way "sensitive to the forms and relations of movements" (Waterman, 2001, p153), meaning they are more inclusive and societal focused in nature than the labour movement in its still institutionalised current form. Rather than focusing on the development and maintenance of institutionalised structures and practices that trade unions have done (ICFTU, 2000), these groups have organised and co-operated using networks and co-operatives built from the bottom-up.

The "formation of networks of many different sorts, local and international" (Bullock, 1994, p121) has allowed organisations such as SEWA to reach workers operating "in a wide variety of sub-sectors" (WIEGO, 2003h, p1) in a fashion that would have proven problematic had a traditional, more rigid structure been adhered to. An attitude prevails that other social movements can provide important resources, ideas or expertise that can assist attempts to support workers. The apparent success gained from such policies in affording workers protection points to a successful implementation of the processes of social movement unionism and subsequently negates a key counter-argument from the labour movement that social movements are not applicable to the world of work.

These organisations have all recognised that it is with grassroots work at "the local level that women can most readily gain a foothold in the structures of negotiating and decision-making power" (Wichterich, 2000, p161). Hence the focus is often placed on working at the most personal levels in order that co- operation and organising takes place, although these organisations do span all levels of action including the global (Waterman, 2001) through co-ordinated action and co-operation.

Grassroots, affirmative action at the workplace, often taken in the form of silent protests such as wearing slogans on clothing (Mort, 1998), takes its place alongside mutual support in the form of "co- operatives ...aimed at social and economic betterment of its members through mutual aid" (Rowbotham and Mitter, 1994, p35) in a policy that follows the trend towards shifts in practice and organisation inherent in social movement unionism. Such a strategy means that not only can workers be organised and contacted with relative ease, but issues are addressed quickly and in full sight of the affected workers rather than behind closed doors in institutionalised discussions. In essence these organisations revert back to the original ethos of the labour movement, that of assisting and supporting fellow workers, rather than of attempting to gain power and influence through institutionalisation.

These 'new' organisations are active not only at the local level, but they also operate on an international scale akin to the internationalism that was shown to be problematic at the national and regional levels of the labour movement. SEWA for example "has been active in lobbying the national and international bodies" (Rowbotham and Mitter, 1994, p40) in an attempt to influence policy making at the very highest levels through its wide range of issue areas such as "urban policies, global markets, organisation and representation and statistics" (WIEGO, 2003h, p1).

Even in such endeavours there is always a conscious effort to maintain a balance between "women inside ...the established political structures and women outside" (Wichterich, 2000, p162) in order that political leverage does not come at the expense of relevancy for members. In this sense there is recognition that fluidity and dynamism that means workers are always the focus, is more important to an effective social movement in the 21st century than strict, institutionalised lines of control. Because these organisations have been developed in the global age of intertwining levels of action, they appear as neither global nor national organisations, and instead have a framework that adapts to context, and facilitates true co-operation between differing organisations.

This highlights that the international dimension means much more than merely working with global institutions in an often restrictive framework, and attempts have been made to forge meaningful links between a variety of groups across the globe, unified by the common aim of gaining societal change (Beck, 2000, pI 66).

In such pursuits it is noticeable that there has been no attempt to universalise issues or narrow the focus of attention of organisations such as that seen in the ICFTU, in order that an agenda may easily cross boundaries. Instead there is a recognition that "diversity is...strength" (Wichterich, 1994, pl46) with conscious effort being made to heed the caveat that "it should not be taken for granted that women, while united by exploitation from patriarchy and capitalism, form a naturally cohesive unit" (Grint, I998, p208). Care has been taken to address the divergent issues facing women and unprotected workers as a whole on the grander stage of world politics and also simultaneously in a local, grassroots manner meaning that workers around the world are truly represented.

Rather than attempting to coalesce divergent perspectives and practices of organisations into a single overarching organisation such as the ETUC, the networks and policies prevalent at the local level are of equal importance at the supranational level to this movement (Wichterich, I994, p 147), and are perhaps more inclusive. Exchanges of information and strategies are commonplace across all levels of the organisations as relevancy, efficiency and effectiveness are maintained at all costs. Whilst networking appears to have succeeded in forging closer links between the various groups around the world, these groups still remain geographically fragmented and scattered. Yet efficient co-operation and co-ordination through, for example, the implementation of global technology (chapter three), means that progress is still possible.

In essence, rather than operating within the confines of what may be seen as traditional political space, these organisations embrace the fluidity and dynamism inherent in the term movement, presenting an alternative to modes of representation and action that find their roots in previous centuries. These organisations highlight that whilst the political structure is important for those operating in GCS, it is not necessary to rely on institutionalised structures and co-ordination with political bodies.

The questions of widening the agenda of the labour movement and building social coalitions, as central to social movement unionism, have been largely rejected by the traditional labour movement. Yet these organisations have pursued such policies to great success, as they "have made alliances with other groups ...[including] environmental lobbyists and campaigners on debt" (Bullock, 1994, p131). By doing so they have assured their increasingly important position within global socio-politics by becoming part of a stronger and more visible whole, unlike the labour movement that has in the past shied away from meaningful coalitions for fear of losing already threatened powers. In doing so, these movements appear to have pushed the traditional labour movement into a make or break situation. Traditional unions face a situation where they have the opportunity to work with and learn from these social women's movements, or instead gradually be made less relevant as more groupings of workers see social movement unionism influenced organising as a viable alternative to traditional trade unions.

Yet despite the successes of these social movement unions, the traditional labour movement remains relatively uninterested. When discussing the issue of the emergence and growing importance of these groups a senior labour movement figure was keen to promote the idea (much as with NGOs) that "just because they are new doesn't mean they are good and democratic"[71]. Rather missing the point, this perspective shows a reluctance to either acknowledge the lessons that can be learned from social movements or to forge links with them in a way that could

---

71. Interview with ICFTU Official, 24/7/2002.

eventually lead to a new global social movement unionism.

Attempting to judge 'new movements' such as SEWA by utilising traditional parameters of understanding such as institutional democracy side-steps one of the central tenets of social movement unionism. Namely that there are a variety of different strategies and policies suitable for different issues areas and peoples, and the existing frameworks for understanding and action are not necessarily the most suitable in all contexts any longer.

Instead of attempting to learn from these new organisations, elements of the labour movement such as "the armed men from the Mexican Labour Confederation" (Rowbotham and Mitter, 1994, p108) who occupied a female dominated garment factory when female led organisation was due to commence, descend into conflict with women. Whilst the situation may not be as volatile all over the world it is nonetheless true that the male dominated traditional labour movement often maintains a defensive posture that hampers any learning of benefits of innovations such as co-operative structures as promoted by women led movements.

If the traditional labour movement remains relatively cut adrift not only from new forms of organisation such as SEWA, but also other social movements, the potential for a recasting of concepts and practices is small. Change cannot be artificially imposed from external sources, so a process of development must take place within the labour movement. There exists at present a framework within which the labour movement may come into contact with other elements of global civil society, in turn naturally learning new ideas and ways of operating without necessarily immediately rejecting existing traditions. This framework is the model of the World Social Forum now discussed.

World Social Forums as the Catalystfor Social Movement Unionism?

The World Social Forum (WSF) first held in 2001 appears as a possible facilitating framework for the development of at least social coalition integral to social movement unionism, as well as the natural meeting of the labour movement with new practices and concepts more applicable for the 21st century. This WSF was organised in response to the world trade forums, with the goal of bringing together the peoples of the world to propose alternatives to Neoliberal globalisation (WCL, 2003). This was not closed off to any grouping within GCS, and had at its heart a true belief that regardless of the movement's goal, there is a genuine and pressing need for a "common expression of revulsion at the neo- liberal order" (WCL, 2003, p1).

Within the WSF, social movements co-operated and discussed issues with all factions of the global labour movement, and the WCL, ICFTU and ETUC managed to create and submit joint statements and proposals on many wide-ranging issues including "the need for decent work...[and] seeking a reform of international institutions" (WCL, 2003, p2). What is critical about the WSF is that it shows how despite prevailing divergent attitudes, there is at least the potential for the labour movement to become more involved with other elements of GCS.

The social forum model has the potential to assist the development of the labour movement because it presents an opportunity for the movement's key assets, namely its expertise in organising, negotiating agreements and operating with key organisations (O'Brien et al eds. 2000, pp77-108) that stems from its institutionalised history, to be used. Therefore it does not represent a complete rejection of practices and structures for the labour movement, meaning those within the movement are not as explicitly threatened as they may fear.

The WSF also presents explicit opportunities for the labour movement and the workers it represents, as social movements of all kinds come into contact with the labour movement in a way that can foster harmonious relations and the groundwork for future co-operation. This occurs in a way that is not necessarily as forced or false as some within the labour movement have appeared sceptical of. Within the confines of this forum model, the WCL and ICFTU are simultaneously allowed to not only negotiate and co-operate together behind closed doors, but may also seek out other elements of GCS that appear compatible with their aims and practices. This provides an organic process that broadens the labour movements perspective and understanding of modern global civil society as new practices and perspectives are encountered.

The creation and maintenance of such social forums does not represent a revolutionary step towards social movement unionism and the immediate transplantation of the labour movement to be the central figure in GCS. Rather it represents an arena within which all involved in GCS may come together, form alliances and most critically, learn from each other. Such a process can at least lead to "new political discourse that will appeal to a critical mass of workers, labour activists and activists from other issue areas" (Stevis and Boswell, 1997, p96) more suited to the 21st century than the present fractured system, as all voices are heard together on an equal footing.

Through increased interactions with newer, more fluid

social movements the labour movement has the opportunity to learn new skills and practices that ensure it can move away from "models developed under a national/industrial/colonial capitalism at a moment in which capitalism is becoming globalised" (Waterman, 1999, p2). But critically, the labour movement will not become simply "an NGO campaigning, lobbying and networking along with the rest of them" (Munck, 1998, p9), as its organisational skills are used not least to facilitate the organisation of the forum model.

Once the forum ends, initiatives and action programmes are taken away by participants and acted on in manners specific to the organisation, with for example, certain social movements organising grassroots action, and the global labour institutions potentially acting as a central hub between civil society and political and institutions due to their capabilities and history (O'Brien et al eds. 2000). Here we see a truly dynamic form of social coalition building that has been so central to the social movement unionist focus of this research.

This process of interaction between the actors of civil society is important as it shows that despite scepticism and stumbling blocks, the labour movement is in a position to develop towards the formation presented by other social movements including the worker's organisations discussed above. The learning of new fashions of "organising and operating" (Fairbrother, 2000, p59) can make social movement unionism so often rejected, an acceptable path of development successful this process can be mirrored at all levels of action from the national to the regional, as perspectives and practices are shifted downwards, from the global level.

Conclusion

This research has analysed the extent to which existing dimensions of the traditional labour movement are developing their practices and policies along the path of social movement unionism as discussed in chapter two. It has been repeatedly shown that scepticism and defensive attitudes have hampered developments, alongside a continued reliance on traditional forms of organising and operating not necessarily best suited to contemporary socio-politics. This concluding chapter has moved to show that at present the global dimension of the labour movement is a divided body that not only continues to often reject the ethos of social movement unionism, but also largely ignores key opportunities.

It has been argued that World Social Forums can provide an arena in which the labour movement may gradually develop new understandings and practices, through increased interaction with other elements of GCS. Amongst those operating in GCS are a series of worker's organisations that provide a tangible test for a form of social movement unionism as they have developed outside the framework of the traditional labour. Without the pre-conceived ideas or entrenched practices that come with the traditions and institutionalisation women have used the very strategies of networking, strategies focusing on human agency, international co-operation and social coalition building that are central to our understanding of social movements operating within GCS. Allied to a militant attitude, such strategies have allowed SEWA, WIEGO and the other new breed of movements to successfully organise, protect and represent workers at all levels in a way that the contemporary labour movement has difficulty in doing.

Through the continuing development of networking forums such as those discussed above, there exists the potential for the labour movement to gain increased linkages to these movements, along with other social groupings. And in doing so there is the possibility that those within the labour movement who have appeared sceptical to new ways of operating and organising could see the real world benefits of such paths of development. Yet to simply try and assimilate these women's movements into the existing labour movement would be a dangerous step that could lead to fracturing, and new more fluid policies provide the answer. The purpose of analysing the women's movements and highlighting their importance is not to simply argue they are a 'blueprint' for other movements, but rather to show that they provide a test for social movement unionism and are worthy of the labour movement's attention.

6. CONCLUSION: A REJECTION OF SOCIAL MOVEMENT UNIONISM?

Foundations of Research

Building upon an initial understanding that social movements may be regarded as a body of persons with a common objective, whose membership and objectives may change, this research had the point of departure that such "unbounded, fluid and mobile" (Amoore and Langley, 2004, p103) forms of socio-political agency are more suited to the modern political economy than forms historically favoured by the labour movement. It is this conceptualisation that builds the foundations for social movement unionism that represents a cumulative shift in practices and processes towards more ground level, societal action in order that labour organisations may become more like social movements (Munck, 1998, p1).

Analysis focused on the historic adoption or rejection of three central elements of social movement unionism: changes to the internal structures and practices of the labour movement, a push towards a more explicitly international focus for the movement, and the development of linkages with other social movements within civil society. Looking at organisations at the national, European regional and global levels, it was asked whether before the financial crisis we saw new attitudes and forms of organisation emerge within the labour movement.

Had there been substantive evidence that social movement unionism was being embraced by those within the labour movement previously, it would suggest foundations may be in place for an effective re-orientation of the labour movement the current period of uncertainty and division. It is such developments that would herald the beginnings of a concerted and planned "process of re-composition of [the] key sectors" (Munck, 1998, p6) of a labour movement weakened by a series of intertwined pressures in the global era. Yet the findings of primary research indicated that optimistic accounts of social movement unionism as given in much academic literature, bore little resemblance to the tangible policies and strategies of unions and related organisations.

Going back 15 years we can see that prevalent attitudes held by the figures within the labour movement suggested an implicit and at times explicit rejection of new and dynamic forms of operating, based upon a hostility towards and mistrust of social movements operating within civil society. Essentially the central hypothesis of social movement unionism, that the traditional labour movement is in need of reinvigoration and new forms of operating, holds true given the substantial pressures presented by globalisation, but if lessons are to be learned from the past, then it is the attitudes and opinions of those working in key positions within labour organisations that will drive or hamper change.

The social movement unionism whose implementation has been tested for throughout was shown in chapter two to be implicitly based on theoretical constructs from a Gramscian perspective, the perspective chosen as the foundation for this research. Hegemony, social forces, the potential for change, civil and political society, the state, and historic blocs are all concepts that provide the framework in which the labour movement operates. Whilst all of these ideas have informed this work and its understanding of moves to gain "political and ideological leadership'; (Simon, 1982, p21) by labour, certain elements of the theoretical framework were shown to be more central for an understanding of social movement unionism

In particular, the social coalition dimension of social movement unionism, whereby co-operation with other social movements is seen as key for the labour movement (Stevis and Boswell, 1997, p96), is based implicitly upon the Gramscian understanding that for a group to succeed in moves towards hegemony or counter-hegemony, it must gain the "consent of other classes and social forces through creating and maintaining a system of alliances by means of political and ideological struggle" (Simon, 1991, p23-24). Mirroring contemporary calls for changes in focus and attitude within the modern labour movement, this shift necessitates a move to address "the interests of other subordinate groups" (Gramsci, 1971, pp181-2) as well as their own relatively narrowly defined interests.

Because the building of such coalitions will take place in civil society, an understanding of this "ensemble of organisms commonly called private" (Gramsci, 1971, pl2) has also been critical to provide insight into developments. In order that this research could provide reliable insights into the international dimension of social movement unionism, the framework extended beyond the regional, nationally oriented Gramscian though to incorporate the neo-Gramscian work of Cox that extended analysis to the global level, allowing an understanding of "what forces may have the emancipatory potential to change or transform the prevailing order" (Bieler and Morton, 2004a, p87) in the modern age.

Chapter three provided a detailed discussion of the major challenges presented in the modern global era, in order that the context in which social movement unionism is places, was given. The processes of the globalisation of production, technology, governance and civil society were argued to be intertwined processes of great importance for the labour movement in the modern global political economy, given the key challenges and in some instances opportunities, that they present the labour movement.

Spurred by the growth in importance of the MNC, it is the globalisation of production that has presented most challenges for labour, presenting increased job insecurity for workers, and often a lowering of workplace protection and standards through "a downward spiral of deteriorated labour standards" (SiD, 1997, p3). And it is the globalisation of technology, including advances in telecommunications and transport capabilities, which have facilitated such shifts in the relations of production.

Subsequently, "intelligent machinery is replacing human beings in countless tasks" (Rifkin, 1995, p3), and similar mechanisation and technologisation leaves many workers with only part time or temporary contracts, technology has presented challenges to labour. Yet technology, through the possibility of a "network structure and the principle of co-operation" (Waterman, 1985, p245) across national borders, has also long presented the labour movement with certain opportunities for new forms of operation and action.

These processes were shown to be taking place within a

context of internationalising governance and indeed civil society. With the nation state remaining critical as an important agent of representation (Featherstone, 1993), as well as a form of global elector and mediator, it was argued that organisations such as the EU and UN represent a certain "internationalisation of the state" (Cox, 1993, p260). With certain political powers being globalised, a central assertion was that a similar globalising of civil society is to be observed and expected. Inherently "distinct from the architecture of states and markets" (Amoore and Langley, 2004, p89) yet not abstracted from them, GCS is a true area of societal contestation within which the labour movement must work towards building a position of strength in the global political economy.

Within GCS we see "networks, new social movements, NGOs, and other informal citizens groups" (Pasha and Blaney, 1998, p425) that could co-ordinate to form a social coalition as envisaged by social movement unionism. It is this dimension of the political economy that for this research, presents an opportunity to open "up new potential for counter-hegemonic and progressive forces to begin to make transnational links, and thereby to insert themselves in a more differentiated, multilateral order" (Gill, 1991a, p311).

The Labour Movement and Social Movement Unionism

The book then moved to analyse what tangible developments may be observed in the structures, practices and attitudes surrounding the labour movement that that could point towards a sustained and coordinated shift in operation on behalf of key labour organisations. Utilising existing material to provide background arguments, the originality and insight of this thesis came from the inclusion of primary data, specifically results from interviews with key labour movement officials within national, regional, and global organisations. It was this primary material that allowed continual analysis of the degree to which existing academic constructs mirror developments occurring across all levels of the labour movement, in order that it could be shown whether new conceptual considerations are needed for future research into labour related issues.

Focusing on the example of Britain for the national level of analysis, it was shown that the period of Conservative governance between 1979 and 1997 presented a series of legislative and social challenges to the efficacy of the labour movement in the modern era. Even in the Labour governed period after 1997, the labour movement was unable to make substantial inroads into a repositioning of itself as a central player in the political economy. With union membership having dropped from 12,639,000 in 1970 to 7,295,000 in 2000 and down to 6.2 million in 2017 (Trade Union Membership Statistical Bulletin, 2017), and unions having long lost their position as a central player in the socio-politics of Britain (McIllroy, 2000), it was expected that new, more dynamic forms of operating akin to social movement unionism would have been adopted.

Yet the reality was somewhat different, with scepticism and negativity apparently hampering any large-scale redevelopment of the labour movement. With visible attempts to develop new ways of operating sometimes amounting to small, ad-hoc policies such as changing "the union logo so that it appeared less masculine"[72], substantive changes in attitude and practice appeared far off if the findings of this research are indicative of wider trends.

Whilst there was an understanding that unions are operating within "European and global markets which affect people's lives"[73], internationalisation did not appear top of most agendas. Even when it is seen as important, avenues of

---

72. Interview with TGWU Official, 9/9/2002.
73. Interview with UNISON Official, 9/9/2002.

internationalisation such as existing organisations and structures are largely ignored. Rather than relying on existing organisations such as the ETUC, unions appear more likely to pursue co-ordination and co-operation in a self-determinate fashion, with linkages between national unions showing that "trade unionism can help people around the world ...and [the] focus should not be narrowly British based"[74].

If attitudes towards internationalisation were often sceptical, portraying a fear of giving up any of their already weakened powers, linkage to social movements was often met with hostility, as it was argued in one case that the labour movement must ensure that any agenda addresses "the world of work and nothing more"[75] . Whilst some were more positive towards elements of social movement unionism, such as the GMB, the reality is often one of scepticism. Social movement unionism as discussed in academic literature was therefore shown to bear little resemblance to the observable path of development foreseen by certain important labour movement policy makers at this level, meaning a new focus may be necessary in future explanations of labour related issues.

---

74. Interview with GMB Official, 27/5/2002.
75. Interview with TGWU Official, 9/9/2002.

The next chapter moved to analyse developments at the European regional level, in a bid to discover whether any more effective moves towards social movement unionism, and an internationalisation of the labour movement were observable. Paying attention to the existing structures of the European level of labour politics, it was argued that a fracturing between organisations hampers an effective Europeanisation of the labour movement. Despite the ETUC, EIFs, and EWCs combining to provide a potential framework for action, there appears to have been a failure to develop a "representational base of mobilisational constituency" (Taylor and Mathers, 2002, p97). A lack of engendering popular support, a historical reliance on political will for progress, and the lack of a credible capital opponent combine to hamper any effective moves towards an international labour movement.

When social movement unionism was addressed at this level, once again scepticism was often observed. Rather than leading a "new internationalism [that] has moved beyond a conception of transnational collective bargaining, involving a more social movement unionism" (Munck, 2002, p254), there were arguments that moves towards a social coalition could lead to "unions be[ing] lumped in with women's groups in an amalgam that will not get anything done"[76]. Such attitudes contribute to a situation where this dimension of labour politics remains apparently divorced from national organisations and workers, and fails to meet the requirements for an effective Europeanisation of the labour movement, particularly whilst there is a continued lack of "popular interest in international solidarity" (Turner, 1996, p326). The central internationalist element of social movement unionism is therefore threatened by the fracturing of a dimension of the labour movement that could provide a co-ordinating 'hub' between global organisations and those at the lower national and regional levels, meaning that further research into the possibilities of future progress towards true Europeanisation is valuable.

Analysis then moved to the global level, to determine whether this would provide a more dynamic, planned and proactive leadership of the labour movement, with the ICFTU and WCL acting as leaders of global labour. Moves towards a united social movement unionist vision for the future of the labour movement at this level seem scuppered when the divisions between these two central organisations are made clear. Following years of animosity stemming from cold war tensions, some within

76. Interview with ETUI Researcher, 23/7/2002.

the ICFTU display a dismissive attitude towards the WCL and see the ICFTIJ as 'natural leader' of the global labour movement 77. In turn, staff were at times eager to suggest a subsuming of the WCL into its own body, contrary to the WCL's argument that it is "dangerous to infer rashly the expediency of a single trade union structure at the international level" (WCL, 2001, p34).

The attitudes held within the ICFTU appeared to reject a social movement unionism that would force them to "think and act outside the straightjacket of [their] traditions" (Jordan, 2000, p2), instead arguing that "the world of work is all that matter and its best we stick to what we know"[78]. This contrasts with the WCL, that is apparently keen to work within a "broader coalition of social forces" (Cox, 2000, p29), with key staff arguing that contacts "with a whole range of NGOs like Human Rights Watch" (WCL, 2001, p 19) add a "youth and freshness to the movement"[79] that is vital in the modern global political economy. This, allied to the relatively positive attitude of the similarly weakened GMB, suggests that many in the labour movement are in denial of the need to adopt new practices, and it is only those most starkly aware of the

---

77. Interview with ETUC Official, 22/7/2002.
78. Interview with ICFTU Official, 24/7/2002.
79. Interview with WCL Official, 24/7/2002

challenges facing them that embrace new practices.

The research then highlighted an important element of the labour movement that is in a sense, a test case of social movement unionism so rejected by traditional organisations. Organisations including SEWA and WIEGO have developed outside the traditional boundaries of the labour movement. In turn they have developed in a way that holds central a way of operating "sensitive to the forms and relations of movement" (Waterman, 2001, p153) rather than a reliance on traditional and outdated methods of action.

From a focus on working at the local level (Wichterich, 2000), to an international focus that allows for effective "lobbying [of] the national and international bodies" (Rowbotham and Mitter, 1994, p40), such organisations represent the formation so far apparently rejected by the traditional labour movement figures interviewed in the process of this research. There is no guarantee that these organisations will prove any more effective than existing labour structures in the long term as they attempt to protect workers from the pressures presented by globalisation, yet their existence is evidence that the traditional labour movement's scepticism towards change as exemplified by social movement unionism is based more on attitudinal problems than tangible evidence that these processes will fail.

The global dimension of this research also highlighted the importance of World Social Forums for providing an arena in which the labour movement may slowly become accustomed to more modern ways of operating. Because of their meeting place nature, WSFs appear to provide a context within which shifts towards learning new ways of operating could occur without organisations facing loss of powers or changes in structures. This is due to how WSFs allow labour organisations to come into contact with more modern and dynamic social movements, in a natural and non-committal fashion.

Increased co-ordination and co-operation with social movements in such a way may allow for the retention of existing structures, alongside the learning of new ways of operating and organising, without them being imposed artificially. Such an organic process seems to point to a situation whereby social movement unionism is gradually learned, meaning that fears held within the labour movement that it will become "an NGO campaigning, lobbying and networking along with the rest of them" (Munck, 1998, p9) are unfounded.

When the global level of the labour movement comes to terms with the importance of social movement unionism, it is seems much more likely that a common vision will be attained, in turn being shifted downwards through the regional and national levels to provide a comprehensive shift in the structures, attitudes, and processes within the movement as a whole. Yet it has been shown that lower levels of organisation and action such as the national level, presently provide organisations apparently much more capable of potentially developing new forms of operating through direct contact with workers, and internationalisation through self-determined linkages between individual trade unions.

The centrality of civil society

A central theme of this research has been the importance of civil society as the arena in which social movement unionism takes place, with unions operating alongside other private and social organisations for societal change. Starting from the Gramscian understanding of civil society as the "ensemble of organisms commonly called private" (Gramsci, 1971, p12), in which "all popular-democratic struggles" (Simon, 1982, p69) take place, this research has moved to discuss the concept on a global scale. Global civil society conceived as a "grassroots but transnational challenge to the realist idea of a nation-state system" (Pasha and Blaney, 1998, p425), is central to understanding the context within which modern labour organisations find themselves operating. Whilst the initial hypothesis of this research was confident of the potential transformative powers held by actors operating within civil society, analysis of the attitudes held by those within trade unions has highlighted a tension between labour organisations and the concept of this "realm of contesting ideas" (Cox, 1999, p4).

Although mindful to not equate civil society with simple coherence or inherent commonality of purpose (Pasha and Blaney, 1998), there is the danger that one can assume a degree of co-operation between those operating within it. Yet analysis of labour organisations' adoption of social movement principles within global civil society challenges our conceptions. Given the constant scepticism and at times explicit hostility towards calls for labour organisations to "reach out to other social movements" (O'Brien, 2000b, p515), it is important to assess whether such attitudes, when held by those within civil society, serve to negate the plurality and diversity of this socio-political realm. In the Gramscian understanding of civil society, it is undeniable that as organisations outside the political structures of the state, labour organisations are civil society actors, yet what affect is there if this substantial element of civil society appears to reject the principles of co-operation, plurality and diversity.

Rather than embracing the opportunity to come into contact with a range of social movements all with the aim of changing the world around us, labour organisations have for the most part rejected such moves with such ferocity at times that the foundations of this construct are in danger of being fractured. When presented with questions of building coalitions with social movements, or even simply building some form of co-operative network, one influential figure within a major labour organisation stated that any extending of operations to incorporate alliances with other social movements was highly unrealistic as "trade unions [are] *the* social movements"[80].

There was no reasoned explanation of why linkages to other social movements was unacceptable either at present or in the future, but rather an argument that the rest of civil society does not matter in the same way as trade unions do. This is a telling insight into the attitudes held within the labour movement, as there is a sense of such string identity and

---

80. Interview with ICFTU Official, 24/7/2002.

feelings that labour organisations are somehow naturally more important, relevant to workers and in a sense, are entitled to a central position within society without necessarily fighting for it, that they threaten any effective widening of remit or linkages to other organisations.

Trade unions, being private organisations, are implicitly part of civil society, but their attitudes force us to acknowledge that some within civil society act in a fashion that challenges traditional theoretical conceptions of an embracing of plurality and openness between societal actors. For labour organisations, if they do indeed see themselves as members of civil society, see themselves as somehow a more valid form of organisation than others, subsequently rejecting true pluralism. If such institutionalised stances are taken by those within civil society, one must question whether our conceptions should shift to address issues of assumed leadership and conflict, as much as co-operation and fluidity. Otherwise there is a risk of attempting to understand the labour movement using conceptual tools that they themselves reject.

Importantly, it appears that those within the labour movement see themselves as natural leaders of civil society, with any other form of social movement being subservient to them. And this is a central implication for future understandings of societal issues, for it is important to understand how in the future such attitudes can be reconciled with a vision of a plural, dynamic space in which leadership goes against dynamism and co-operation.

Hostility shown by the labour movement towards other elements of civil society was not confined to any particular level of analysis. Instead it cut across all levels from the national to global. This highlights a critical tension that exists between the need for the labour movement to extend its ways of operating to incorporate social coalitions as posited by academics, and the implicit desire of those operating within the labour movement to retain their positions as the leaders of anything that pertains to societal action surrounding workers.

Essentially, the labour movement at present operates in an institutionalised fashion, with attitudes and structures that mean discussions of social movement unionism, based on grassroots challenges and global civil society, are irreconcilable with reality. Future research must acknowledge this fracture between existing conceptualisations and tangible issues, and develop an understanding of civil society that allows for exclusion, elitism and issues of leadership to be analysed. In doing so it is entirely possible that civil society would be conceived not simply as a contested realm, but rather as a fractured, multi-layered realm in which differing forms of organisation and movement operate at differing levels according to goals, composition, and histories.

The changing nature of labour

It is also clear that we need to change how the term labour is discussed. Having identified and analysed not only the challenges presented to the labour movement, but also the framework in which labour organisations operate, it is clear that it is no longer satisfactory to narrowly conceive of worker's interests as being tied to a particular conception of work. Instead it is vital that those within the labour movement, as well as academic commentators, recognise that in the modern global political economy the interests of workers extend into new spheres of human security, including the environment, gender and race, issues addresses within the WSF.

This research has also highlighted the need to shift our conceptions of what is termed labour, beyond traditional perspectives. The multidimensional nature of labour highlighted early in this research, is an important element of our understanding of real world labour politics. For only through an explicit understanding that all meanings of labour are extended and challenged in the global age, can one effectively understand the possibilities for resistance and action. Yet the findings of this research show that such academic conceptions do not necessarily match tangible attitudes and practices surrounding the contemporary labour movement.

Whilst when discussions focused on the human aspect of the term labour, there was an understanding held by some in the labour movement that a narrow conception of what is termed labour is no longer valid, this was a rare acknowledgement. All too often the reality was that those operating within the labour movement are still focused on an understanding of labour that is rooted in the past, as concrete policies to attract women, migrant, and ethnic minority workers are minimal at best, or lack ground level support.

Discussions with those within the labour movement served to show how conceptions of work and workers were for the most part firmly rooted in a more traditional conception of an ill-defined workplace. When pushed on the conception of the workplace held by each major labour organisation, there was some confusion, as it appeared that little thought had been given to how work had changed in recent years. That key members of labour organisations were unsure as to what arena they were actually focusing on, served to further highlight the need for increased clarity and innovation in our discussions of the world of work.

Again, those within the labour movement ignore the plurality and diversity of societal issues that is apparent when using academic constructs of civil society and socio-political action. This continued ignorance on behalf of the traditional labour movement threatens to undermine how we conceive of social movement unionism, for again there is a fracture between what is discussed in academic literature, and what is empirically observable in the global political economy. Rather than discussing shifts in union practice and organisation in terms of a labour movement in need of redevelopment and re-composition in a rough-shod fashion that ignores the existing conceptions and practices of the labour movement, future research should try to understand the defensive and at times hostile attitude taken by those who see their positions as being threatened.

Adopting such a strategy of analysis serves to highlight the possibility that due to the combination of prevailing practices that are in need of change, and attitudes that hamper such change, existing forms of labour organisation are more unsuited to contemporary forms of socio-politics than is at first hypothesised. In this instance an implication is that future research could more explicitly focus on the rise of entirely fresh and new forms of labour organisation, and their suitability for growth and development, rather than their use as a model and tool for traditional labour organisations.

Existing labour organisations must come to terms with an increasingly diverse membership that challenges what we think of as being a traditional worker. The need for change is amplified when we consider how new conceptions of what the term work means are needed. Work and in turn labour extends far beyond traditional concerns regarding a singular workforce and workplace, as may have been the case in previous ages of heavy industry.

With a fracturing of traditional working class identities bringing new workers such as women, migrants and ethnic minorities into focus, so an understanding of the extension of the workplace and multiplicity of issues at stake for modern labour must be addressed by those attempting to understand social movement unionism. With labour being composed of many societal groupings, and spatial boundaries no longer defining where work is carried out as for example the home is a place of work, it is inevitable that our conception of labour must extend into new dimensions of human security.

For social movement unionism and the necessarily intertwining constituencies of social movements and labour organisations, alerts us to how issues including the environment, racial divisions, gender equality, and indeed in the era of global terrorism, more traditional conceptions of security, all impact upon workers. Extending the concept of labour to include this acknowledgement not only addresses the issues of globalisation more adequately, but also fulfils the Gramscian requisite that for hegemony to be attained, a groups focus must extend beyond "narrow corporate interests...[and] transcend the corporate limits of the purely economic class, and can and must become the interests of other subordinate groups too" (Gramsci, 1971, pp181-182).

Although this research has highlighted the need for such a widening of focus, it has also highlighted again, a rejection or ignorance of such moves on behalf of the labour movement. Instead there has been a prevailing argument on behalf of many organisations that the focus of action for the labour movement must "pertain to the world of work and nothing more"[81], an attitude not only sceptical and defensive, but also outdated given that fact that this world of work is at best ill-defined. This failure to engage in discussion on a widening of the remit for labour organisations is inextricably linked to a rejection of linkages to other social movements, suggesting an entrenched and defensive attitude that hampers progress.

Yet there are examples of unions addressing issues that for many are seen as the domain of someone else. Both the GMB union in Britain and the WCL at the global level expressed an interest in looking beyond mere workplace matters, arguing that all issues are complementary in the end[82]. This shows again that those aware of the challenges facing them are willing to look beyond their traditional frameworks of understanding to find new partners for action, and new issues that they may be able to secure gains in, in a hope that ultimately their leverage as a legitimate social actor in the eyes of both the public and political- economic bodies will benefit.

This research therefore leads to an argument that implementation of social movement unionism must incorporate analysis and understanding of all societal issues, not due to

---

81. Interview with TGWU Official, 27/6/2002.
82. Interview with GMB Official, 27/5/2002

"woolly political correctness"[83] but because in the modern world labour extends across all society. Given that workers are also citizens and family members and social actors, it is necessary in the future to further understand the degree to which labour is intertwined with wider issues. Further analysis of this could provide even more compelling reasons for the adoption of social movement unionism by labour organisations, and further highlight the need for increased linkages between these and other social movements. Yet a future focus on the relationship between labour organisations and social movements is not simply a tool to understand how strength can be gained in order that 'real issues' surrounding work can be addressed, but rather because to do otherwise is to focus on issues that are increasingly marginalised in the diverse and pluralistic society.

The need for multi-level understanding

It is now unsatisfactory to conceive of socio-political structures, organisation, or action as taking place within a specific dimension of the global political economy. Instead, analysis must acknowledge that key sites of contestation and agency are

---

83. Interview with TGWU Official, 11/2/2002.

intertwined and detailed understanding must take into account such dynamics.

The previous understanding that the social movement unionism debate should address a multiplicity of issues not out of a mechanistic urge to 'use' them, but rather through an understanding of the intertwining nature of the global political economy, reinforces an attitude that analysis and action at one level is not enough. This research has made explicit how challenges presented to the labour movement overlap from the local to the global levels, highlighting a multi-layered political economy that social movement unionism must acknowledge. To talk of global pressures, then to focus on national, regional or global responses and forms of governance is invalid and lacks insight. Instead the true picture is one in which the processes of globalisation affect all workers at all levels, in which all labour organisations at all levels are intertwined whether they know it or not, and in which the structures of governance present a multi-layered framework in which social movement unionism takes place.

Those analysing social movement unionism should attempt to understand not just an internationalisation of the labour movement, but also the possibilities for a truly coordinated labour movement. Such a labour movement would have linkages, frameworks and forms of operating that work both from the top-down and vice- versa, to address issues that extend across geographical boundaries, within a framework afforded not only by the globalisation of civil society challenged by the attitudes of labour organisations, but also through the globalisation of the state. Yet despite presenting the initial conceptual frameworks surrounding such multi-layered analysis, this research has also gone on to observe how any developments towards multi-layered operating in the labour movement appear fractured.

Academic debate surrounds the extent to which the state is losing centrality within the global political economy yet in reality we see a multi-layered framework of governance comprising local, national, regional, and global organisations. Social movement unionism should reject calls that the state is waning or that traditional political frameworks are not suited to our understanding of contemporary politics, and instead highlight the multi-faceted nature of this framework and its potential for labour. Yet despite some within the labour movement acknowledging the importance that "every level:

global, regional, national, and sub regional and community"[84] have for workers and the labour movement, the true situation is one of issues and structures still being seen as compartmentalised according to their geographical position.

At present, local councils, national governments, regional bodies such as the EU, and global organisations such as the G-groupings, all create a co-ordinated political framework of governance, yet this is often ignored by academic discussions of social movement unionism and the labour organisations that research focuses on. The reality is that this framework of governance ensures that the global economy currently presenting challenges to labour is regulated, and in turn this presents a framework of governance that the labour movement may interact with. Yet whilst there exists the potential for a coordinated framework for national trade unions, regional organisations such as the ETUC, and global organisations including the WCL and ICFTU, to work together with directives and inspiration emanating from the global level, a fractured mix of associations has been shown to threaten progress.

---

84. Interview with GMB Official, 27/5/2002

Those at the national level show little interest in, or understanding of, institutions and action and the European or global levels. Whilst the European level is beset by a series of stumbling blocks in the way of an effective Europeanisation of labour. And in turn the global dimension of the labour movement is beset by conflict. Essentially, each organisation is primarily and almost exclusively concerned with issues at its own level, unless tangible and immediate benefits are to be had. It is incumbent on future research to extend analysis beyond such conceptions to understand the truly multi-layered nature of social and political action within the modern global political economy, in order that the hesitancy towards change on behalf of the labour movement is understood, and a viable vision for future action may be developed.

Unions and Social Movements

As well as these more theoretical implications, this research has also highlighted other issues more directly tied to the relationship between the labour movement and social movement unionism. Throughout this research a central theme has been the exploration of the central dynamic between unions, social movements, and civil society. Rather than being built upon inclusion and co- operation, this relationship was shown to be often based on attitudes of hostility, scepticism, and fracture held by central figures within the labour movement. There are three central issues that serve to highlight the implications of this dynamic for future research regarding social movement unionism and issues surrounding the labour movement as a whole. The first of these, surrounding the self-perception of labour organisations, presents perhaps the biggest tension between traditional labour organisations and social movements. For many of those positioned within the traditional labour movement hold a conception that presents a fracture between themselves and social movements, seeing unions as somehow more valid forms of organising than other social movements. A common attitude expressing hostility towards organisations such as NGOs was that they do not have the "democratic accountability"[85], of labour organisations, and the latter can be seen as the "genuine social movements"[86].

The reality seems that the labour movement is concerned with speaking on behalf of its members, and indeed, the whole of society, without necessarily being in a position to do so. Yet all too often the membership that unions claim to exclusively represent, is neither as substantial as was once the case, nor as

---

85. Interview with TUC Official, 27/6/2002.
86. Interview with ETUC Official, 22/7/2002.

representative of wider society, precisely due to the changes in the world of work that social movement unionism addresses. Short sighted arguments from the labour movement show a reluctance to enter into a true form of social movement unionism. Fear of being "lumped in with women's groups in an amalgam that will not get anything done"[87] hampers collaboration. An attitude that organisations such as the ETUC have a true "representative capacity for society in Europe"[88] that is lacking in other organisations within civil society, is symptomatic of a mistaken attitude held across the whole of the labour movement, that as long as they exist, they are somehow natural societal leaders.

That there is such determination to retain sole responsibility for the representation of a particular element of society is dangerous, as the pressures of 5 true obstacles to widespread redevelopment of labour movement action could be based more on prejudice and fear than tangible and understandable concerns. Yet the main objectives of modern labour organisation, namely to increase and widen membership, address issues outside a traditional understanding of the world of work, and to regain legitimacy in the eyes of a global public

---

87. Interview with ETUI Researcher, 23/7/2002.
88. Interview with ETUC Official, 22/7/2002.

to a great extent disenchanted with traditional politics, would surely be better served through interactions promoted by social movement unionism.

Increased participation alongside social movements to address issues across all society was seen to be very much the exception to the rule in the course of this research. Two examples are co-operation between unions and social movements are the recent Stop the War coalition in Britain, and work undertaken between international labour organisations and social movements in the Clean Clothes Campaign.

What is apparent is that the organisations with which co-operation took place could be seen as major organisations, so unions could rest assured that these organisations including Oxfam, Greenpeace were 'legitimate'. But there is also the issue that it seemed those in the labour movement would be reluctant to undertake such action if they felt their position as 'leader of all labour' was under threat. Yet there is no reason that such co-operation cannot occur between the labour movement and other, perhaps smaller social movements, now there are concrete examples of successful partnerships to look back at. It appears that the main obstacle, as has been shown throughout this research, is scepticism and prejudice on behalf of the labour movement.

At present it is undeniable that the traditional labour movement has suffered greatly in the face of a series of intertwined pressures in the global age, and that as yet it has failed to completely address all the issues it faces. Because of this the labour movement analysed in this research has been shown to be in a weakened state of influence, in need of a coordinated framework for renewal and redevelopment.

Whilst it is true that social movement unionism, developed within a framework of intertwined levels of organisation including the national, regional and global, could address many issues, this research has repeatedly highlighted the various attitudinal and structural stumbling blocks that lie in the way of such a development.

The fact is that future research must implicitly understand the negativity shown towards substantial shifts in policy and strategy, in order that future academic work does not appear as completely divorced from tangible developments in the same manner as some commentary does. A final implication for future research is the role which new forms of labour organisation could play in the development of a social movement unionism either incorporating existing labour organisations, or by way of replacing them.

By looking to relatively new forms of labour organisation in the form of SEWA and WIEGO and others, one can see a real world test for social movement unionism that the labour movement as a whole may be able to learn from. With their development taking a path "sensitive to the forms and relations of movements" (Waterman, 2001, p153), these organisations are based on principles of networking, grassroots organisation and action, internationalisation, and building "alliances with other groups" (Bullock, 1994, p131). It is conceivable that the importance of these organisations will not come from a transferring of principles and practices onto the traditional labour organisations, but rather through a natural process of acknowledgement on behalf of the latter. Yet a simple wait and see policy is not enough, either for the labour movement as a whole, or for researchers wishing to understand more about labour in IPE.

A more proactive agenda is necessary, with attention being shifted to understanding the reasons for the success of these new forms of labour organisations. Such inquiry on behalf of academics and those in the labour movement could explicitly highlight the tangible reasons behind any calls for substantial changes in action or structure for the labour movement.

Another element of the political economy that could prove a central element of the future agenda of the labour movement, without necessitating immediate rejection of past practices and attitudes, are WSFs. The WSFs appear as possible 'facilitating frameworks' for the development of social networking that could lead to the natural embracing of new techniques and concepts by the labour movement. Based upon a "common expression of revulsion at the neo-liberal order" (WCL, 2003, p 1), these forums may prove enticing to traditional labour organisations and figures due to their non-binding nature that for some may make them appear as meaningless.

Yet the true worth of such meetings is an unknown quantity that can only be measured in the future. The potential for these to provide a solid new agenda for labour organisations is clear however, as increased and regular contact with other elements of civil society will widen perspectives to acknowledge a range of issues currently seen as outside the remit of an effective labour movement.

Through increased focus on meaningful participation in WSFs, the labour movement could develop a wider conception of the issues that are applicable to workers and work in the global political economy, and the degree to which social movements could prove valuable partners in socio-political action. With such an agenda focusing on global organisations, it is possible that ideas and practices could filter down throughout the levels of action. It is for this reason that an increased analysis of WSFs and the role that labour organisations play in them is necessary. For by combining analysis of this, as well as an increased understanding of new labour organisations and their linkages with more traditional unions, it is possible that those discussing social movement unionism will be able to point towards concrete possibilities for its development, rather than concrete obstacles that hamper it.

Appendix A. INTERVIEWS CONDUCTED

All interviews lasted between one and two hours. They were conducted one on one and were structured around a planned interview question plan. Answers were recorded in note form and transcribed immediately after the interview. Because of the sensitive nature of many comments made, the identities of interviewees are kept confidential.

GMB Official,	Newcastle upon Tyne.	27/5/2002
UNISON Official,	Newcastle upon Tyne.	9/9/2002.
TGWU Official,	Newcastle upon Tyne.	9/9/2002.
TUC Official,	London.	27/6/2002.
GMB official,	London.	12/9/2002.
TUC Official,	London.	11/9/2002.
TUC Official,	London.	11/12/2002.
IGTLWF Official,	Newcastle upon Tyne.	7/8/2002.
ETUC Official, Brussels.		22/7/2002.
ETUC Official, Brussels.		22/7/2002
ICFTU Official,	Brussels.	24/7/2002.
ICFTU Official,	Brussels.	22/7/2002.
WCL Official,	Brussels.	24/7/2002.
ETUI Researcher	Brussels.	23/7/2002.

Appendix B. THE HISTORY, GOALS, PRACTICES AND STRUCTURE OF SEWA

History of SEWA[89]

SEWA is a trade union first registered in India in 1972, focusing its attention on the organisation of poor, self-employed women workers. Those most likely to be members are self-employed women, argued by SEWA to earn a living through their own labour or small businesses. They are specifically eligible for SEWA membership if they do not obtain regular salaried employment with welfare benefits like workers in the organised sector. The need for this form of labour organisation is made clear when one recognises that such workers constitute some 93% of the total Indian labour force, with some 94% of women working within the informal economy.

SEWA originated from the Textile Labour Association (TLA), India's oldest and largest union of textile workers founded in 1920. The inspiration for this union came from the socio-political action of Mahatma Gandhi, who led a successful strike of textile workers in 1917. Believing that positive organised strength of workers could be developed by awakening

---

[89]. This appendix is an adapted version of various self-portrayal documents found at http://www.sewa.org.

the consciousness inherent in all workers, Gandhi argued that by developing a common unity as well as individual and collective personality, worker should be able to resist oppression and exploitation from the state or employer. Critically for the contemporary issue of social movement unionism, Gandhi and the labour organisations he inspired, believed that a union's remit should cover all aspects of worker's lives both in the factory and at home, and not just narrowly defined issues pertaining to an ill-defined world of work.

Deriving inspiration from such arguments, in 1954 the Women's Wing of TLA was created. Initially focused on training and welfare activities pertaining to the lives of specific elements of the workforce including female mill workers, by 1968 the organisation provided classes in sewing, knitting embroidery, spinning, press composition, typing, and stenography in centres throughout the city for the wives and daughters of mill workers.

In the early 1970s, it became apparent that despite the obvious successes of this labour organisation in assisting women workers in India, there were still large proportions of the female workforce suffering from exploitation by contractors. Further investigation highlighted the vast numbers of self-employed workers who were untouched by union legislation. In 1971, a small group of migrant women working as cart-pullers approached the TLA for assistance in finding housing, and after discussions with these workers, the leader of the TLA decided that the issues facing self-employed women meant that a dedicated organisation was necessary.

Having brought the plight of workers to the attention of the press, and following disputes with contractors, popular will amongst women workers led to the creation of SEWA in December 1971. Despite there being no real history of self-employed workers organising themselves in the form of a trade union, it was decided that as a workers' association, SEWA should indeed establish itself as a Trade Union. This led to a struggle for SEWA to obtain official recognition as Trade Union, as the Labour Department refused to register SEWA as since there was no recognised employer, the workers would have no one to struggle against. Importantly for our contemporary conception of what constitutes labour politics, SEWA successfully argued that a union was not necessarily against an employer, but was for the unity of the workers.

Growing continuously from 1972, SEWA has continually increased in its membership as well as the number and diversity of occupations within its remit. Despite conflict with the organisation that created it, leading to expulsion from the TLA in 1981, SEWA has grown faster than other social organisations in India, and has started a vast array of new initiatives. Specifically, those within SEWA are keen to point out the importance of new cooperatives, a more militant trade union attitude, and the many supportive services it offers its workers.

Goals

SEWA's main goals to this day are to organise women workers in order to attempt to obtain full employment, and that workers are able to be self-reliant. SEWA argues that poor women's growth, development and employment is best afforded when they have work and income security and food security. It also occurs when they are healthy, able to access childcare and have a roof over their heads. In order to ensure that the organisation is moving towards the attainment of the two central goals of Full Employment and self-reliance, constant monitoring and evaluation is required. Members have developed ten key questions that assist the evaluation of progress and success. These questions pertaining to the situations of workers are:

- Have more members obtained more employment?
- Has their income increased?

- Have they obtained food and nutrition?

- Has their health been safeguarded?

- Have they obtained child-care?

- Have they obtained or improved their housing?

- Have their assets increased? (e.g. Their own savings, land, house, work-space, tools or work, licenses, identity cards, cattle and share in cooperatives; and all in their own name).

- Have the worker's organisational strength increased?

- Has worker's leadership increased?

- Have they become self-reliant both collectively and individually?

Campaigns, Organising and Services

The central aims of SEWA are to assist workers in the struggle against constraints and limitations imposed on them by society and the economy, with additional development activities aiming to strengthen women's bargaining power and offer them new alternatives to existing forms of precarious employment. Practically, strategies are carried out through the joint action of unions and co- operatives. Rather than attempting to gain power and influence as more traditional labour organisations do, SEWA is instead ruled by the principles of 'satya' (truth), 'ahimsa' (non-violence), 'sarvadharma' (integrating all faiths, all people) and 'khadi' (propagation of local employment and self-reliance).

Critically for this research and any other research that aims to understand the role that organisations such as SEWA play in the future development of the labour movement, SEWA argues that it is both an organisation and a movement. Rather than focusing on influencing political and economic institutions, SEWA is focused on societal change and support. SEWA has been described by those working within its structure as a 'sangam', or confluence of three movements: the labour movement, the co-operative movement and the women's movement, a model which harshly contrasts with the structures of labour organisations examined in this thesis that dismiss the very notion of social movement unionism. By promoting co-operation and action, SEWA believes that self-employed workers can create and develop their own movement that allows their economic and social contributions to become recognised across society.

Facing the pressures of globalisation identified in this research, SEWA believes that there are both new opportunities as well as threats to some traditional areas of employment. Critically, moves towards increased participation within international frameworks of organisations and co-operation point towards an internationalisation of this labour movement in the same vein as social movement unionism argues for.

Having begun organising rural workers in the late 1970s, difficult circumstances have forced SEWA to learn harsh lessons and inventive ways of operating within the political economy. Understanding that the basis of obtaining higher wages is the capacity and power to bargain, yet many workers do not have such capacity due to their lack of reliable employment, SEWA has moved the focus towards organising women and supporting them in building their own workers' organisations, and organising mass mobilisation of workers. Such mass mobilisation that brings issues to the attention of a wide section of society is carried out as part of a campaign focusing on clearly identified issues. These issues are identified not by committees of bureaucrats, but rather by and local leaders who are able to see which issue affects large numbers of people, which affects them deeply, or is felt as unjust or intolerable and is continually called to attention. Specific elements of campaigning and mobilisation have included:

- Moves towards increasing employment opportunities for women and thus increasing women's bargaining power.

- Developing women's assets in order that they are not dependent on poorly paid, unreliable jobs.

- Capacity-building and leadership development of rural women so that they are in charge of their own destiny.

- Providing food & social security so that those without employment are safe.

- Encouraging self-reliance for women both in economic terms and in terms of running their own economic organisations.

- Ecoregeneration through employment for rural women in order that the areas in which workers live are not destroyed.

In the late 1990s there were ten major campaigns organised around pressing issues such as these affecting SEWA members. These campaigns, which spread through networks of co-operation and information sharing, were:

- Food security campaign

- Construction worker's campaign

- Forest workers' campaign

- Campaign for recognition of unorganised sector workers

- Campaign for a right to child care

- Minimum wages campaign

- The clear Ahmedabad (City) campaign

- Campaign for the recognition of midwives

- The water campaign

- Social Movement Unionism? Analysis of Labour Organisation's Strategies in the Global Political &onomy

- Home based worker campaign

- Vendors campaign

As well as organising campaigns such as these, and providing other assistance one may expect from a union, SEWA also provides a series of support initiatives that are somewhat different to the formalised services offered by the traditional labour organisations analysed in this thesis. Supportive services like savings and credit, health care, child care, insurance, legal aid, capacity building and communication services are important needs of poor women according to SEWA, and accordingly the organisation has helped women take a number of initiatives in organising these services for themselves and their SEWA 'sisters'. These services are most often provided in a decentralised and affordable manner, essentially at the doorsteps of workers. Of further significance is how supportive services can be and are themselves a source of self-employment for those involved. For example, midwives may charge for their services and crèche workers collect fees for taking care of young children.

As such, these services do not appear simply as charity, for women are ready to pay for the services in a manner that results in the financial viability of the supportive services. In addition, some supportive services like savings and credit, health and child care have formed their own co-operatives, leading to self-sufficiency and the propagation of social movement unionist principles amongst a whole new subset of workers. The central support services provided and supported by SEWA are:

- SEWA bank
- Health care
- Child care
- Work security insurance
- Legal services
- Capacity building of SEWA members
- Housing and infrastructure
- Video SEWA

Structure and Membership

A two-tier level of governs SEWA elected representation, with the members of each specific trade electing their representatives by a ratio of 1 representative per 100 members. These representatives then form the Trade Council (Pratinidhi Mandai), in addition and parallel to Trade Committees (Dhandha Samiti) representing the interests of each trade. The Trade Committees have no fixed proportion to number of members but varies between 15 and 50 members, and meet every month to discuss specific problems relating to their workers. Every three years the Trade Council elects an Executive Committee of 25 members, and the representation on the Executive Committee reflects the proportion of the membership. The office-bearers of the trade union are elected from the Executive members, and it has become a practice to elect the President from the trade with the largest membership.

SEWA members are specifically workers who have no fixed employee-employer relationship and depend on their own labour for survival. They are argued to be especially at risk due to their often poor and illiterate nature. Yet these workers are extremely economically active, and contribute to the creation of some 64% of GDP of India. SEWA identifies three key types of self-employed women workers:

- Hawkers, vendors and small business women like vegetable, fruit, fish, egg and other vendors of food items, household goods and clothes vendors.

- Home-based workers like weavers, potters, 'bidi' and 'agarbatti' workers, 'papad' rollers, ready-made garment workers, women who process

- Agricultural products and artisans.

- Manual labourers & servıce providers like agricultural labourers, construction workers, contract labourers, handcart pullers, head-loaders, domestic workers and Laundry workers.

Appendix C. GOALS, PROGRAMMES AND STRUCTURE OF WIEGO

Background and Goal [90]

Women in Informal Employment: Globalizing and Organizing (WIEGO) is a worldwide coalition of institutions and individuals concerned with improving the status of women in the economy's informal sector. The coalition was born out of the conviction that women workers, particularly those from low-income households, are concentrated in the informal sector. Although the informal sector contributes to both poverty alleviation and economic growth it remains largely invisible in official statistics and policies as was argued in this thesis. Thus, WIEGO strives to improve the status of the informal sector through compiling better statistics, conducting research and developing programmes and policies. WIEGO's name reflects two of its major concerns:

- Women informal workers are an integral part of a globalising economy; and
- Women workers need to organise at local and international

---

[90]. This Appendix was adapted from various self-portrayal documents found at http://www.wiego.org

levels in order to respond effectively to the new opportunities - as well as the negative impacts - associated with global trade and investment

WIEGO was established in 1997. Founding members currently serve on the Steering Committee and include representatives from three different types of organisations:

- Grassroots organisations
- Research or academic institutions
- International development organisations including SEWA, Harvard University and UNIFEM.

WIEGO commissions background issues papers to identify key programme, research, and policy issues. Planning workshops take place where key grassroots, research, and policy actors convene to help frame issues more precisely and formulate plans of action. Component activities of each programme include a mix of research studies, programmatic interventions, and policy dialogues. Project funds for undertaking these activities are raised independently or jointly and go directly to collaborating institutions or individuals from various countries.

Programme Areas

For each of its five work programme areas, WIEGO commissions issues papers to identify programme, research and policy priorities. It then convenes workshops of grassroots, research and policy actors. Collaborating institutions and individuals undertake component activities. The key five programme areas are:

- Urban Policies.

  The WIEGO Urban Policies Programme works to correct the public policy bias against street vendors and establish their right to vend. The programme also works to improve services for street vendors and helps them to organise themselves and present their concerns to city planners.

- Global Markets.

  The Global Markets Programme analyses the impact of globalization and trade liberalisation on women workers and producers, particularly home- based workers, to highlight where threats can be minimised and new economic opportunities seized.

- Social Protection.

  Recognising that most informal sector workers have no access to social protection systems, WIEGO's programme promotes innovative approaches, such as micro-finance, to provide social protection to women workers in the informal sector.

- Organisation and Representation.

  WIEGO works with grass roots organisations and international networks of informal workers, such as Homenet and StreetNet to strengthen organising capacity and to increase the visibility and voice of women in the informal economy. WIEGO also works with international trade union organisations and tries to put informal sector workers on the agenda of governments and international organisations.

- Statistics.

    WIEGO has been working closely with the United Nations Statistics Division and ILO Bureau for Statistics on this programme. It sponsored the preparation of papers for the international Expert Group on Informal Sector Statistics and commissioned reports on linkages between the informal Sector, poverty and gender. It is also working with the Economic Commission for Africa to produce estimates of the informal sector for national accounts in African countries. It works with SEWA on a project to estimate the size and economic contribution of the informal sector in India and with national statistical institutes in Africa, Asia and Latin America.

Appendix D. WORLD SOCIAL FORUM

Founding Principles[91]

The World Social Forum is argued to be not an organisation, nor a united front platform, but rather" ...an open meeting place for reflective thinking, democratic debate of ideas, formulation of proposals, free exchange of experiences and inter-linking for effective action, by groups and movements of civil society that are opposed to neo- liberalism and to domination of the world by capital and any form of imperialism, and are committed to building a society centred on the human person" (From the WSF Charter of Principles). In this sense it provides a forum for discussion, co-operation and learning for labour organisations.

Background to WSF

Peoples' movements around the world are working to demonstrate that the path to sustainable development, social and economic justice lies in alternative models for people-centred and self-reliant progress, rather than in neo-liberal globalisation. It is

---

[91]. This appendix was adapted from various documents found at http://www.wsfindia.org

these movements that compose the WSFs. The WSF was created to provide an open platform to discuss strategies of resistance to the model for globalisation formulated at the annual World Economic Forum at Davos by large multinational corporations, national governments, IMF, the World Bank and the WTO, which are the foot soldiers of these corporations.

Firmly committed to the belief that Another World Is Possible the WSF is an open space for discussing alternatives to the dominant neo-liberal processes, for exchanging experiences and for strengthening alliances among mass organisations, peoples' movements and civil society organisations. The first WSF was held in 2001 in the southern Brazilian City of Porto Alegre. It was here that the WSF's Charter of Principles was adopted to provide a framework for the forum. The annual forums in 2002 and 2003 saw the movement grow rapidly, as the WSF came to symbolise the strength of the anti-globalisation movement and became a rallying point for worldwide protest against the American invasion of Iraq.

At WSF 2002, it was proposed that the next forum be held outside Brazil. This shift represents the need that the WSF process must reach out in a larger way to the African-Asian region, where two-thirds of the world's population lives. The

Asian Social Forum in Hyderabad in January 2003 was a demonstration of India's commitment to the WSF process, prompting suggestions that the next be held in the subcontinent. A preparatory meeting at Bhopal in April 2002 framed the Bhopal Declaration, which governs the WSF process in India. The organisational outline of the process governing the form to be held in India was also formulated.

The WSF India process reached its peak in Mumbai between January 16 and January 21, 2004, when 75,000 delegates were expected to express their belief that 'Another World Is Possible'.

Charter of Principles

The committee of Brazilian organisations that conceived of and organised the first World Social Forum, held in Porto Alegre from January 25th to 30th, 2001, after evaluating the results of that Forum and the expectations it raised, consider it necessary and legitimate to draw up a Charter of Principles to guide the continued pursuit of that initiative. While the principles contained in this Charter - to be respected by all those, who wish to take part in the process and to organise new editions of the World Social Forum- are a consolidation of the decisions that presided over the holding of the Porto Alegre Forum and ensured its success, they extend the reach of those decisions and define orientations that flow from their logic.

- The World Social Forum is an open meeting place for reflective thinking, democratic debate of ideas, formulation of proposals, free exchange of experiences and interlinking for effective action, by groups and movements of civil society that are opposed to neo-liberalism and to domination of the world by capital and any form of imperialism, and are committed to building a planetary society directed towards fruitful relationships among Mankind and between it and the Earth.

- The World Social Forum at Porto Alegre was an event localised in time and place. From now on, in the certainty proclaimed at Porto Alegre that "Another World Is Possible", it becomes a permanent process of seeking and building alternatives, which cannot be reduced to the events supporting it.

- The World Social Forum is a world process. All the meetings that are held as part of this process have an international dimension.

- The alternatives proposed at the World Social Forum stand in opposition to a process of globalisation commanded by the large multinational corporations and by the governments and international institutions at the service of those corporations' interests, with the complicity of national governments. They are designed to ensure that globalisation in solidarity will prevail as a new stage in world history. This will respect universal human rights, and those of all citizens - men and women - of all nations and the environment and will rest on democratic international systems and institutions at the service of social justice, equality and the sovereignty of peoples.

- The World Social Forum brings together and interlinks only organisations and movements of civil society from all the countries in the world, but intends neither to be a body representing world civil society.

- The meetings of the World Social Forum do not deliberate on behalf of the World Social Forum as a body. No one, therefore, will be authorised, on behalf of any of the editions of the Forum, to express positions claiming to be those of all its participants. The participants in the Forum shall not be called on to take decisions as a body, whether by vote or acclamation, on declarations or proposals for action that would commit all, or the majority, of them and that propose to be taken as establishing positions of the

Forum as a body. It thus does not constitute a locus of power to be disputed by the participants in its meetings, nor does it intend to constitute the only option for interrelation and action by the organisations and movements that participate in it.

- Nonetheless, organisations or groups of organisations that participate in the Forum's meetings must be assured the right, during such meetings, to deliberate on declarations or actions they may decide on, whether singly or in co-ordination with other participants. The World Social Forum undertakes to circulate such decisions widely by the means at its disposal, without directing, 'hierarchising', censuring or restricting them, but as deliberations of the organisations or groups of organisations that made the decisions.

- The World Social Forum is a plural, diversified, non-confessional, non-governmental and non-party context that, in a decentralised fashion, interrelates organisations and movements engaged in concrete action at levels from the local to the international to build another world.

- The World Social Forum will always be a forum open to pluralism and to the diversity of activities and ways of engaging of the organisations and movements that decide to participate in it, as well as the diversity of genders, ethnicity, cultures, generations and physical capacities, providing they abide by this Charter of Principles. Neither party representations nor military organisations shall participate in the Forum. Government leaders and members of legislatures who accept the commitments of this Charter may be invited to participate in a personal capacity.

- The World Social Forum is opposed to all totalitarian and reductionist views of economy, development and history and to the use of violence as a means of social control by the State. It upholds respect for Human Rights, the practices of real democracy, participatory democracy, peaceful relations, in equality and solidarity, among people, ethnicity, genders and peoples, and condemns all forms of domination and all subjection of one person by another.

- As a forum for debate the World Social Forum is a movement of ideas that prompts reflection, and the transparent circulation of the results of that reflection, on the mechanisms and instruments of domination by capital, on means and actions to resist and overcome that domination, and on the alternatives proposed to solve the problems of exclusion and social inequality that the process of capitalist globalisation with its racist, sexist and environmentally destructive dimensions is creating internationally and within countries.

- As a framework for the exchange of experiences, the World Social Forum encourages understanding and mutual recognition amongst its participant organisations and movements, and places special value on the exchange among them, particularly on all that society is building to centre economic activity and political action on meeting the needs of people and respecting nature, in the present and for future generations.

- As a context for interrelations, the World Social Forum seeks to strengthen and create new national and international links among organisations and movements of society, that, in both public and private life, will increase the capacity for non-violent social resistance to the process of dehumanization the world is undergoing and to the violence used by the State, and reinforce the humanising measures being taken by the action of these movements and organisations.

- As a context for interrelations, the World Social Forum seeks to strengthen and create new national and international links among organisations and movements of society, that, in both public and private life, will increase the capacity for non-violent social resistance to the process of dehumanisation the world is undergoing and to the violence used by the State, and reinforce the humanising measures being taken by the action of these movements and organisations.

- The World Social Forum is a process that encourages its participant organisations and movements to situate their actions, from the local level to the national level and seeking active participation in international contexts, as issues of planetary citizenship, and to introduce onto the global agenda the change-inducing practices that they are experimenting in building a new world in solidarity.

APPROVED AND ADOPTED IN SAO PAULO, ON APRIL 9, 2001, BY THE ORGANISATIONS THAT MAKE UP THE WORLD SOCIAL FORUM ORGANJZATJNG COMMITTEE, APPROVED WITH MODIFICATIONS BY THE WORLD SOCIAL FORUM INTERNATIONAL COUNCIL ON JUNE 10, 2001.

Mobilisation in the WSF

Mobilisation for the World Social Forum encompasses a broad variety themes and diverse groups of people, organisations, groups, and networks on a global scale. In their diversities and complexities, all those involved in the forums agree that 'Another World Is Possible'. Operating at both the local and the global levels, the WSF is simultaneously specific and universal, and mobilisation reflects that. On one hand, WSF brings people together to fight for their own sectoral and regionally specific causes. On the other, it also brings people together on a common understanding of the necessity of united and global struggle for change. Hence, mobilisation needs to concentrate on groups own causes whilst also seeking to increase unity and global approaches to common issues.

Not only an event, but also a process, mobilisation for those within the WSF is not a mere act of one-time, physical mobilisation of human beings, but is an ongoing process of exchange of ideas converging around a planetary approach to bring about a world free of exploitation, oppression, exclusion, and discrimination. Those operating within the WSF are proud to argue that it is an open process full of opportunities. This is exemplified by the way WSFs comprise hundreds of conferences, seminars, workshops, round tables, testimonials, panel discussions, exhibitions, and cultural events. Opportunities are available for groups to engage in vertical interactions as well as the creation and development of horizontal alliances, both nationally and globally. Cross-region, cross-country, cross-continent dialogue and exchange of information and ideas is a unique feature of the WSF. The mobilisation group sees itself as holding a great collective responsibility to reach out to the people from India and across the world to mobilise to ensure maximum representation of issues, sectors, and peoples' movements across the globe.

REFERENCES

Ackers, P. Smith, C. and Smith, P (eds.) (1996) *The New Workplace and Trade Unionism: critical perspectives on world and organisation.* (New York, Routledge)

Adamson, W. L. (1980) *Hegemony and Revolution, a Study of Antonio Gramsci's Political and Cultural Theory.* (London, University of California)

Addison, J. T. and Burton, J. (1984) *Trade Unions and Society: Some Lessons of the British Experience.* (Columbia, The Fraser Institute)

Adkin, L. (1999) Ecology and Labour: Towards a New Societal Paradigm. In Munck, R. and Waterman, P. (eds.) (1998) *Labor Worldwide in the Era of Globalization: alternative union models in the new world order.* (Basingstoke, Macmillan)

Amin, A and Goddard, J. B. (eds.) (1986) *Technological Change, Industrial Restructuring and Regional Development.* (London, Unwin Hyman)

Amin. A. (eds.) (1994) *Globalization, Institutions and Regional Development in Europe.* (Oxford, Oxford University Press)

Amoore, L. (2002a) *Globalisation Contested: an International Political Economy of Work.* (Manchester, Manchester University Press)

_____ (2002b) Work, Production and Social Relations: Repositioning the Firm in the IPE. In Harrod, J. and O'Brien, R. (eds.) (2002) *Global Unions? Theory and Strategies of Organized Labour in the Global Political Economy.* (London, Routledge)

Amoore, L. and Langley, P. (2004) Ambiguities of Global Civil Society. *Review of International Studies,* 30:1.

Anderson, B. (2000) *Doing the Dirty Work? The Global Politics of Domestic Labour.* (London, Zed Books)

Auerbach, S. (1990) *Legislation for Conflict.* (Oxford, Clarendon Press)

Angeli, E. and Murphy. C. (eds.) (1988) *America's Quest for Supremacy and the Third World.* (London, Pinter)

Axford, B. (1995) *The Global System: Economics, Politics and Culture.*
(Cambridge, Polity Press)

Bacon, N and Storey, J. (2000) New Employee Relations Strategies in Britain: Towards Individualism or Partnership? *British Journal of Industrial Relations,* 38:3.

Baglioni, G and Crouch, C. (eds.) (1990) *European Industrial Relations, the Challenge of Flexibility.* (London, Sage)

Baldwin-Edwards, M. and Arango, J. (eds.) (1999) *Immigrants and the Informal Economy in Southern Europe.* (London, Frank Cass)

Bansbach, M. (2001) Recent German Publications on Industrial Relations at European Level. *European Journal of Industrial Relations,* Vol. 7 No. 1.

Barry Jones, R. J. (1995) *Globalisation and Interdependence in the International Political Economy, Rhetoric and Reality.* (London, Pinter)

Bauman, Z. (1998) *Globalisation, the Human Consequences.* (Cambridge, Polity Press)

Beck, U. (1992) *Risk Society, Towards a New Modernity.* London, Sage

_____ **(2000)** *What is Globalisation?* (Cambridge, Polity Press)

Berenard, M. (2000) Post Fordism and Global Restructuring. In Stubbs, R. and Underhill, G. R. D. (eds.) (2000)

Beynon, J. and Dunkerley, D. (eds.) (2000) *Globalisation: The*

Reader. (The AthelonePress)

Bieler, A. (2001) *Labour and the Struggle against Neo-Liberal Globalisation: a Conceptualisation of Trade Unions' Possible Role at the International.* Paper Prepared for Presentation at ISA Convention, 2001.

Bieler, A. and Morton, A. D. (2004a) A Critical Theory Route to Hegemony, World Order and Historical Change: Neo-Gramscian Perspectives in International Relations. *Capital and Class,* 2004, Spring.

_____ (2004b) *Theoretical and Methodological Challenges of neo-Gramscian Perspectives in Innernational Political Economy.* International Gramsci Society Online. http: www.italnet.nd.edu/gramsci

Birch, K. and Denemark, R. A. (eds.) (1997) *Constituting IPE: IPE Yearbook, vol. 10.* (London, Lynne Reinner)

Blaschke, S. (2000) Union Density and European Integration: Diverging Convergence. *European Journal of Industrial Relations,* Vol. 6 No.2.

Boggs, C. (1984) *The Two Revolutions: Gramsci and the Dilemmas of Western Marxism.* (Bath, The Pitman Press)

Boyer, R. (ed.) (1996) *States Against Markets: The Limits of Globalization.* (London, Routledge)

Brah, A. Hickman, M. J. and Mac and Ghaill (eds.) (1999) *Global Futures: Migration, Environment and Globalization.* (London, Macmillan)

Brown, W. Deakin, S. and Ryan, P. (1997) The Effects of British Industrial Relations Legislation 1979-1997. *National Institute Economic Review, Jul-v 1997.*

Buci-Glucksmann, C. (1980) *Gramsci and the State.* (London, Lawrence and Wishart)

Bullock, S. (1994) *Women and Work.* (London, Zed Books)

Burnham, P. (1991) Neo-Gramscian Hegemony and the International Order.
Capital and Class, v.45 1991.

Cammack, P. (2001) *Making Poverty Work,* unpublished paper.

Caparaso, J. A. and Levine, D.P. (1992) *Theories of Political Economy.*
(Cambridge, Cambridge University Press)

Carter, B. and Poynter, G. (1999) Unions in a Changing Climate: MSF and UNISON Experiences in the New Public Sector. *Industrial Relations Journal, 30.*

Castells, M. (1998, 2000 2nd Ed.) *The Information Age: Economy, Society and Culture Vol. 3: End of Millennium.*
(Oxford, Blackwell)

Cerny, P. G. (1990) *The Changing Architecture of Politics: Structure, Agency, and the Future of the State.* (London, Sage)

Chapman, K. and Humphreys, G. (eds.) (1987) *Technological Change and Industrial Policy.* (Oxford Basil, Blackwell)

Charlwood, A. (2002) Why do Non-Union Employees Want to Unionise? Evidence from Britain. *British Journal of Industrial Relations, 40:3, Sep 2002.*

Chase-Dunn, C. (1989) *Global Formation: Structures of the World Econom_Y.*
(Oxford, Basil Blackwell)

Christi nsen, J, Kostinen, P and Kovalainen, A. (eds.) (1999) *Working Europe, Reshapzng European employment systems.*
(Aldershot, Ashgate)

Colas, A. (2002) *International Civil Society: Social Movements in World Politics.*
(Cambridge, Polity)

Colgan, F. and Ledwith, S. (eds.) (2002) *Gender, Diversity and Trade Unions: International Perspectives.* (London, Routledge)

Cook, J. Roberts, J. and Waylen, G. (eds.) (2000) *Towards a Gendered Political Economy.* (London, MacMillan)

Cox, R. W. (1981) Social Forces, States and World Orders: Beyond International Relations Theory. *Millennium: Journal of International Studies, vol10, No 2.*

_____(1983) Gramsci, Hegemony and International Relations: An Essay in Method. *Millennium: Journal of International Studies, vol12, No 2.*

_____ (1987) *Production, Power and World Order: Social Forces in the Making of History.* (New York, Columbia University Press)

_____ (1993) *Structural Issues of Global Governance: Implications for Europe.* In Gill, S. (ed.) (1993)

_____ (1999) Civil Society at the tum of the millennium: Prospects for an Alternative World Order. *Review of International Studies. 25:1.*

_____ (2000) *Political Economy and World Order: Problems of Power and Knowledge at the Turn of the Millennium.* In Stubbs, R. and Underhill, G. R. D (eds.) (2000)

Cox, R. W. and Schechter, M.G. (2002) *The Political Economy of a Plural World: Critical Reflections on Power, Morals and Civilization.* (London, Routledge)

Crane, G. T. and Amawi, A. (eds.) (1997) *The Theoretical Evolution of International Political Economy; A Reader.* (Oxford, Oxford University Press)

Dale, G. and Cole, M. Eds. (1999) *The European Union and Migrant Labour.*
(Oxford, Berg)

Daniel, W. W. (1987) *Britain's Relative Economic Decline,
1870-1995.*
(London, Pinter)

Degryse, C. (2002) *European Social Dialogue: A Mixed
Picture.* (Brussels, ETUI)

Demart, L. (2000) *Trade Unions and NGOs-Common Causes.*
(Brussels, ICFTU)

Dicken, P. (1992) *Global Shift: The Internationalisation of
Economic ActivitY.*
(Paul Chapman, London) ·

_____ (1998) *Global Shift: Transforming the World
Economy.* (London, Paul Chapman)

Dolvik, J. E. (1997) *Redrawing Boundaries of Solidarity?
ETUC, Social Dialogue and the Europeanisation of Trade
Unions in the 1990s.* In Gabaglio, E and Hoffman, R. (eds.)
(1998)

_____ (1999) *An Emerging Island? ETUC, Social
Dialogue and the Europeanisation of the Trade Unions in the
1990s.* (Brussels, ETUI)

Donaghy, R. (1995) *Trade Unions and Equal Opportunities* in
Shaw, J. and Perrons, D. (eds.) (1995)

Donovan, Lord. (1968) *Report of Royal Commission on Trade
Unions and Employer Associations.* (London, HMSO, Cmnd
3623)

Drainville, A. C. (1994) International Political Economy in the
age of open Marxism. *Review of International Economy, 1 (1).*

Dunford, M. and Perrons, D. (1983) *The Arena of Capital.*
(London, MacMillan)

Ebbinghaus, B. (2002) Trade Union's Changing Role:

Membership Erosion, Organisational Reform, and Social Partnership in Europe. *Industrial Relations Journal, 33:5.* (Oxford, Blackwell)

Economist, 10 September 1994.

Edwards, P. et al. (1998) *Great Britain: From Partial Collectivism to Neo-Liberalism to Where?* In Ferner, A and Hyman, R. (eds.) (1998)

Fairbrother, P. (2000) British Trade Unions Facing the Future. *Capital and Class, Summer 2000 issue 7.*

Falk, R. (1998) Global Civil Society: Perspectives, Initiatives, Movements.
Oxford Development Studies 26:1.

_____ **(2000)** *Resisting 'Globalization-From-Above' Through 'Globali:ation-From-Below.* In Gills, B. K. (ed.) (2000)

Fantasia, R. (1988) *Cultures of Solidarity. Consciousness, Action, and Contemporary African Workers.* (Los Angeles, University of California Press)

Featherstone, M. (1993) Global and Local cultures In **Bird, J. et al (eds.) (1993)** *Mapping the Futures: Local Culture, Global Change.* (London, Routledge)

Femia, J. V. (1981) *Gramsci's Political Thought, Hegemony, Consciousness and the Revolutionary Process.* (Oxford, Clarendon)

Fernandez Kelly, M.P. (1989) International Development and Industrial Restructuring: The Case of Garment and Electronic Industries in Southern California. In **MacEwan, A. (1989)** *Instability and Change in the World Economy.* (New York, Monthly Review Press)

Ferner, A and Hyman, R. (eds.) (1992) *Industrial Relations and the New Europe.* (Oxford, Blackwell)

_____ **(1998)** *Changing Industrial Relations in Europe.* (Oxford, Blackwell)

Financial Times, September 30th 1998.

Fosh, P. and Heery, E. (eds.) (1990) *Trade Unions and Their Members.*
(London, MacMillan).

Gabaglio, E and Hoffman, R. (eds.) (1998) *The ETUC in the Mirror of Industrial Relations Research.* (Brussels: ETUI)

Gallin, D. (1994) Inside the New World Order: Drawing the Battle Lines. *New Politics, Summer, 1994.*

_____ (2001) *Propositions on Trade Unions and Informal Employment in Times ofGlobalisation.* In **Waterman, and Wills, J. (eds.), (2001)**

Gamble, A. (1988) *The Free Economy and the Strong State, The Politics of Thatcherism.* (London, MacMillan Education)

Gamble, A. and Wright, T. (eds.) (1999) *The New Social Democracy.* (Oxford, Blackwell)

Germain, R. and Kenny, M. (1998) Engaging Gramsci: international relations theory and the new Gramscians. *Review of International Studies, 24:3, 21.*

Giddens, A. (1990) *The consequences of modernity.* (Cambridge, The Polity Press)

Gill, S. (1990) *American Hegemony and the Trilateral Commission.* (Cambridge Cambridge University Press) '

_____(1991) *Historical Materialism, Gramsci and International Political Economy* In **Murphy, C. and Tooze, R. (eds.) (1991)**

_____(1991a) Reflections on Global Order and Sociohistorical Time. *Alternatives, vol16, No 3.*

_____(eds.) (1993) *Gramsci, Historical Materialism and*

International Relations. (Cambridge, Cambridge University Press)

_____ (1995) Globalisation, Market Civilisation, and Disciplinary Neoliberalism. *Millennium: Journal of International Studies, 25:3, 1995.*

_____ (eds.) (1997) *Globalization, Democratization and Multilateralism.* (London, MacMillan)

Gills, B. K. (2000) *Globalization and the Politics of Resistance.* (Basingstoke, Macmillan)

_____(2001) Forum: Perspectives on New Political Economy, Re-Orienting the New (International) Political Economy. *New Political Economy, vol. 6, No 2*

Gilpin, R. (1987) *The Political Economy of International Relations.* (Princeton, Princeton University Press)

Gobin, C. (1994) *The European Trade Union Movement and Collective Bargaining at the European Level.* In **Gabaglio, E and Hoffman, R. (eds.)** *(1998)*

Gollbach, J. and Schulten, T. (2000) Cross-Border Collective Bargaining Networks in Europe. *European Journal of Industrial Relations. Vol. 6 No.2*

Gordon, M. and Turner, L. (eds.) (2000) *Transnational Co-operation Among Labor Unions.* (New York, Cornell University Press)

Gramsci, A. (1971) *Selections from the Prison Notebooks.* (London, Lawrence and Wishart)

Gray, A. (1998) New Labour-New Labour Discipline. *Capital and Class, Summer 1998 issue 65.*

Grint, K. (1998) *The Sociology of Work 2nd Ed.* (Oxford, Blackwell)

Groux, G.·Mouriaux, R. and Pernot, J. M. (1993) *The*

Europeanisation of the Trade Unzon Movement: The ETUC. In Gabaglio, E and Hoffman, R. (eds.) (1998)

Guardian, February 3rd, 1999.

Harris, N. (1995) *The New Untouchables: Immigration and the New World Worker.* (London, Penguin)

Harrod, J. and O'Brien, R. (eds.) (2002) *Global Unions? Theory and Strategies of Organized Labour in the Global Political Economy.* (London, Routledge)

Harrod, J. (1987) *Power, Production and the Unprotected Worker.* (New York, Columbia University)

_____(2002) *Towards an International Political Economy of Labour.* In Harrod, J. and O'Brien, R. (eds.) (2002)

Harvey, D. (1989) *The Urban Experience?* (Oxford, Basil Blackwell)

_____(2001) *Spaces of Capital, Towards a Critical Geography.* (Edinburgh, Edinburgh Uni Press)

Hayworth, N. and Hughes, S. (1997) Trade and International Labour Standards: Issues and Debates over a Social Clause. *Journal of Industrial Relations, vol. 39, No 2: 179-195.*

_____ (2000) Internationalism, IR Theory and International Relations. *Journal of Industrial Relations, No 2, June 2000: 195- 213.*

Healy, G. and Kirton, G. (2000) Women, Power and Trade Union Government in the UK. *British Journal of Industrial Relations, 38:3, Sep 2000.*

Beery, E. (2002) Partnership Versus Organising: Alternative Futures for British Trade Unionism. *Industrial Relations Journal, 33:1.*

Held, D. McGrew, A. Goldblatt, D. and Perraton, J. (eds.) (1999) *Global Transformations, Politics, Economics and Culture.* (Cambridge, Polity Press)

Henderson, J. (1989) *The Globalisation of High Technology Production: Society, Space and Semiconductors in the Restructuring of the Modern World.* (London. Routledge)

Herod, A. (ed.) (1998) *Organizing the Landscape, Geographical Perspectives on Labor Unionism.* (Minneapolis University of Minnesota Press)

Hirst, P. (1997) *From Statism to Pluralism. Democracy, Civil Society and Global Politics.* (London, UCL)

Hodson, R. (ed.) (1997) *Research in the Sociology of Work. Vol. 6 The Globalisation of Work.* (London, Jai Press)

Hoffman, R. (2000) *European Trade Union Structures and the Prospects for Labour Relations in Europe,* In **Waddington, J. and Hoffman, R.** (eds.) (2000)

Hoffman, J. and Hoffman, R. (2001) *Globalization: Risks and Opportunities for Labor Policy in Europe.* (Brussels, ETUI)

Hoogvelt, A. (1997) *Globalization and the Postcolonial World: The New Political Economy of Development (Second Edition).* (Basingstoke: Palgrave)

Howells, J. and Wood, M. (1993) *The Globalisation of Production and Technology.* (London, Belhaven)

Hughes, S. and Wilkinson, R. (1998) International Labour Standards and World Trade: No Role for the WTO? *New Political Economy, vol 3, No 3, 1998.*

Humbert, M. (ed.) (1993) *The Impact of Globalisation on Europe's Firms and Industries.* (London, Pinter)

Hyman, R. (1997) The Future of Employee Representation. *British Journal of Industrial Relations, 35:3, Sep 1997.*

_____(1999) National Industrial Relations Systems and Transnational Challenges: An Essay in Review. *European Journal of Industrial Relations, Vol. 5, No.1.*

_____(2001) The Europeanisation-or the Erosion-of Industrial Relations.
Industrial Relations Journal, 32:4.

Hyman, R. and Ferner, A. (eds.) (1994) *New Frontiers in European Industrial Relations.* (London, Blackwell)

Hyman, R. and Streeck, W. (1988) *New Technology and Industrial Relations.*
(Oxford, Basil Blackwell)

Jakobsen, K. A. (2001) Rethinking the International Confederation of Free Trade Unions and its Inter-American Regional Organization. *Antipode, vol 33, No 3.*

Jakubowski, F. (1976) *Ideology and Superstructure in Historical Materialism.* (London, Allison and Busby)

Jenson, J. Hjagen, E. and Reddy, C. (eds.) (1988) *Feminization of the Labour Force, Paradoxes and Promises.* (Cambridge, Polity Press)

Jenson, J. Laufer, J. and Maruani, M. (eds.) (2000) *The Gendering of Inequalities: Women, Men and Work.* (Aldershot, Ashgate)

Kagarlitsky, B. (1995) *The Mirage of Modernization.* (New York, Monthly Review Press)

_____ (1999) *New Realism, New Barbarism; Socialist Theory in the Era of Globalisation.* (London: Pluto)

Kaviraj, S. and Khilnani, S. (eds.) (2001) *Civil Society, history and possibilities.* (Cambridge, Cambridge University Press)

Keane, J. (2003) *Global Civil Society.* (Cambridge, Cambridge University Press)

Keller, B. and Bansbach, M. (2001) Social Dialogues: Tranquil Past, Troubled Present and Uncertain Future. *Industrial Relations Journal, 32:5*

Kelly, J. (1988) Trade *Unions and Socialist Parties.* (London,

Verso)

_____ (1996) *Union Militancy and Social Partnership,* In
Ackers, P. Smith,C. and Smith, P. (eds.) (1996)

_____ (1997) Industrial Relations: Looking to the Future.
British Journal of Industrial Relations, 35:3, Sep 1997.

Keohane, R. 0. (1984) *After Hegemony: Co-operation and
Discord in the World Political Economy.* (Princeton, Princeton
University Press)

Keohane, R. 0. and Milner, H. V. (eds.) (1996)
Internationalization and Domestic Politics. (Cambridge,
Cambridge University Press)

Kessler, S. and Bayliss, F. (1998) *Contemporary British
Industrial Relations, 3'd
Ed.* (London, MacMillan Business)

Kiely, R. (1998) Globalisation, post-fordism and the
contemporary context of development. *International sociology,
vol. 13, No 1, March, 1998.*

Kirton, G. and Greene, A. (2002) The Dynamics of Positive
Action in UK Trade Unions: The Case of Women and Black
Members. *Industrial Relations Journal,
33:2.*

Krugman, P.R. (1994) *Rethinking International Trade.*
(Cambridge, MIT)

Kusnet, D. (1998) *The "America Needs a Raise" Campaign: The
New Labour Movement and the Politics of Living Standards,* In
Mort, J. (ed.) (1998)

Labour Market Trends. (2002) *National Statistics Feature:
Trade Union Membership, an Analysis of Data from the
Autumn 2001 LFS.* July 2002 pp343- 354.

Leacock, E. and Safa, H. I. (eds.) (1986) *Women's Work.*

Development and the Division of Labor by Gender. (London, Bergin and Garvey)

Lecher, W. (1991) *Outlines of a Structure for the European Industrial Relations as seen from the Trade Union Standpoint.* In Gabaglio, E and Hoffman, R. (eds.) (1998)

Lecher, W. and Rub, S. (1999) The Constitution of European Works Councils: From Information Forum to Social Actor? *European Journal of Industrial Relations, Vol. 5 No. 1.*

Le Queux, S. and Fajertag, G. (2001) Towards Europeanization of Collective Bargaining?: Insights from the European Chemical Industry. *European Journal of Industrial Relations, Vol. 7 No. 2.*

Lipschutz, R. D. (1992) Reconstructing World Politics: The Emergence of Global Civil Society. *Millennium, Vol. 21 No. 3.*

Luard, E. (1983) *The management of the world economy.* (London, MacMillan)

Machin, S. (2000) Union Decline in Britain. *British Journal of Industrial Relations, 38:4, Dec 2000.*

Marchand, M. R (2000) *Gendered Representations of the Global: Reading/Writing Globalisation,* In Stubbs. R. and Underhill. G. R. D (eds.) (2000)

Marchand, M.H. and Runyan, A. S. (eds.) (2000) *Gender and Global Restructuring: Sightings, Sites and Resistences.* (London, Routledge)

Marsh, D. (1990) Public Opinion, Trade Unions and Mrs Thatcher. *British Journal of Industrial Relations, 28.*

_____ (1992) *The New Politics of British Trade Unionism, Union Power and the Thatcher Legacy.* (London, MacMillan)

Martin, A. (1999) *Wage Bargaining Under EMU: Europeanisation, Re-Nationalization or Americanization?* (Brussels, ETUI)

Martin, A and Ross, G. (1997*)*, *European Integration and the Europeanisation of Labour.* In **Gabaglio, E and Hoffman, R.** (eds.) (1998)

Martin, A. and Ross, G. (1999) *The Brave New World of Labour.* (New York, Berghahn)

Martin, R. Sonley, P. and Wills, J. (1996) *Union Retreat and the Regions: the Shrinking Landscape of Organized Labour.* (London, Jessica Kingsley)

Mclllroy, J. (1999) Unfinished Business- The reform of strike legislation in Britain. *Employee Relations, Vol. 21, No 6, 1999*

_____ (2000) The New Politics of Pressure- The Trade Union Congress and New Labour in Government. *Industrial Relations Journal, 31:1.*

Milkman, R. (1997) *Farewell to the factory, Autoworkers in the Late Twentieth Century.* (London, University of California)

Miller, D. (1987) *Material Culture and Mass Consumption.* (Oxford, Blackwell)

Mittelman, J. H. (eds.) (1997) *Globalisation, Critical Reflections.* (London, Lynne Rienner)

Mittelman, J.H. (2000) *The Globalisation Syndrome Transition and Resistance.* (Chichester, Princeton)

Mohammadi, A. et al (eds.) (1997) *International Communication.* (University of Minnesota Press)

Moody, K. (1997) *Workers in a Lean World: Unions in the International Economy.* (London, Verso)

Mort, J. (ed.) (1998) *Not Your Father's Union Movement, Inside the AFL-C/0.* (London, Verso)

Monck, R. (1998) *Labour in the Global: Discourses and Practices.* www .antenna.nl/papers

_____(2002) *Globalisation and Labour, The Great Transformation.* (London Zed Books)

Monck, R. and Waterman, P. (eds.) (1998) *Labor Worldwide in the Era of Globalization.* (London, Macmillan)

Murphy, C. (1998) Understanding IR: Understanding Gramsci. *Review of International Studies,* 24.

Murphy, C. (2000) Global Governance: Poorly Done and Poorly Understood. *International Affairs, 76:4.*

Murphy. C. and Tooze. R. (eds.) (1991) *The New International Political Economy.* (Basingstoke, MacMillan)

Novitz, T. (2002) A Revised role for Trade Unions as Designed by New Labour: The Representation Pyramid and Partnership. *Journal of Law and Society, Vol. 29, Number 3, Sep 2002.*

O'Brien, R. Goetz, A.M. Scholte, J. A. and Williams, M (eds.) (2000) *Contesting Global Governance, Multilateral Economic Institutions and Global Social Movements.* (Cambridge, Cambridge University Press)

O'Brien, R. (1999) *Labour and the Study of IPE.* Discussion Paper for University of Newcastle. IPEG Annual Workshop.

_____ (2000a) *The Agency of Labour in a Changing Global Order.* In Stubbs. R. and Underhill. G. R. D (eds.) (2000)

_____ (2000b) The Difficult Birth of a Global Labour Movement. *Review of International Political Economy, vol. 7, No 3.*

_____ (2000c) Workers and World Order. The Tentative Transformation of the International Union Movement. *Review of International Studies, 26:4.*

Oesterheld, W. and Olle, W. (1978) *The Internationalisation of Trade Unions in Western Europe and the Development of the ETUC.* In Gabaglio, E and Hoffman, R. (eds.) (1998)

Ohmae, K. (1996) *The End of the Nation State.* (London,

Harper Collins)

Overbeeck, H. (ed.) (1993) *Restructuring Hegemony in the Global Political Economy, The Rise of Transnational Neo-liberalism in the 1980s.* (London, Routledge)

Overbeeck, H. (2002) Neoliberalism and the Regulation of Global Labour Mobility. *ANNALS, AAPSS, 581.*

Overbeeck, H. and Van Der Pijl, K. (1993) *Restructuring Capital and Restructuring Hegemony: Neo-Liberalism and the Unmaking of the Post War Order.* In Overbeeck, H. (ed.) (1993)

Ozaki et al (eds.) (1992) *Technological Change and Labour Relations.* ILO, New York.

Panitch, L. (1994) Globalisation and the State. *Socialist Register 1994.*

_____ (2001) *Class and Inequality: Strategy for Labour in the Era of Globalisation.* Key Theme Panel, ISA convention, 2001.

Panitch, L. Leys, C. Gregory, A. and Coates, D. (eds.) (2000) *Working Classes Global Realities.* (London, Merlin)

Parker, J. (2000) *Women's Equality in British Qi:lions: The Roles and Impacts of Women's Group Organising.* Unpublished PhD. Thesis, University of Warwick, June.

_____ (2002) Women's Groups in British Unions. *British Journal of Industrial Relations, 40:1, Mar 2002.*

Pasha, M. K. and Blaney, D. L. (1998) Elusive Paradise: The Promise and Peril of Global Civil Society. *Alternatives, 23:3.*

Patel, P. and Pavitt, K. (1991) Large Firms in the Production of the World's Technology: An Important Case of Non-Globalisation. *Journal of International Business Studies, No 22, pp 1-21.*

Phizacklea, A. and Wolkowitz, C. (1995) *Homeworking Women. Gender, Racism and Class at Work.* (London, Sage)

Porter, T. (2000) *The North American Free Trade Agreement.* In Stubbs, R. and Underhill, G. R. D (eds.) (2000)

Radice, H. (1999) Taking Globalisation Seriously. *The Socialist Register, 1999:4, pp1-25.*

Randall, V. and Waylen, G. (eds.) (1998) *Gender, Politics and the State.* (London, Routledge)

Regini, M. (eds.) (1992) *The Future of Labour Movements.* (London, Sage)

Rifkin, J. (1995) *The End of Work; The Decline of the Global Labor Force and the Dawn of the Post-Market Era.* (New York: G.P. Putman's Sons)

Rowbotham, S. and Mitter, S. (eds.) (1994) *Dignity and Daily Bread, New Forms of Organising Among Poor Women in the Third World and the First.* (London, Routledge)

Rubery, J. Smith, M. Fagan, C. and Grimshaw, D. (1998), *Women and European Employment.* (London, Routledge)

Ruigrok, Wand Van Tulder, R. (1995) *The Logic of International Restructuring.* (London: Routledge)

Runyan, A. S. (1997) *Of Markets and Men: The (Re) Making (s) of IPE,* In **Burch, K. and Denemark, R. A. (eds.) (1997)** *Constituting International Political Economy.* (London, Lynne Rienner)

Rupert, M. (1993) *Alienation, Capitalism and the Inter-State System: Towards a Marxian/Gramscian Critique.* **In Gill, S. (ed.) (1993)**

_____(1995) *Producing Hegemony: The Politics of Mass Production and American Global Power.* (Cambridge: Cambridge University Press)

_____ (2000) *Ideologies of Globalisation: Contesting Visions of a New World Order.* (London, Routledge)

Schuerman, W. E. (2001) US Advocacy of Transnational Labour Protections.
Review of International Political Economy, 8:3, Autumn 2001

Shaw, M. (1994) *Global Society and International Relations.* (Cambridge, Polity Press)

_____(1997) *The Theoretical Challenge of Global Society.* In Sreberny- Mohammai, A. et ai (eds.) (1997).

Shaw, J. and Perrons, D. (eds.) (1995) *Making Gender Work, Managing Equal Opportunities.* (Buckingham, Open University Press)

Showstack Sassoon, A. (1987) *Gramsci's Politics.* (London, Hutchinson)

Simon, R. (1982) *Gramsci 's Political Thought: An Introduction.* (London, Lawrence and Wishart)

Simon, R. (1991) *Gramsci 's Political Thought: An Introduction.* Edition Completely Revised. (London, Lawrence and Wishart)

Singh, M. (1990) *The Political Economy of Unorganised Industry, a Study of the Labour Process.* (London, Sage)

SIW. (1997) *Women and the Globalisation of the World Economy.* (London, SIW)

Sklair, L. (1991) *Sociology of the Global System.* (London, Harvester Wheatsheat)

_____ (2001) *The Transnational Capitalist Class.* (Oxford, Blackwell)

Smith, P. (1999) Exclusion and Disarticulation: The Transport and General Workers' Union in the Road Haulage Industry, 1979-1998. *British Journal of Industrial Relations, 37:4, Dec 1999.*

Smith, P. and Morton, G. (2001) New Labour's Reform of Britain's Employment Law: The Devil is Not Only in the Detail But in the Values and Policy Too. *British Journal of*

Spencer, S. (ed.) (1994) *Immigration as an economic asset: The Gennan Experience.* (London, Trentham Books)

Stalker, P. (2000) *Workers Without Frontiers. The Impact of Globalization on International Migration.* (London, Lynne Reinner)

Starr, A. (2000) *Naming the Enemy: Anti Corporate Movements Confront Globalisation.* (London, Zed Books)

Stevis, D. (1999) *Competing (Inter)nationalisms: States, Capitals, and Unions in North American and European Integration.* (Colorado State University)

Stevis, D. and Boswell, T. (1997) Labour: From National Resistance to International Politics. *New Political Economy, vol. 2, No 1, 1997.*

_____ **(2001)** *International Labour Organisation, 1960s to the Present: not just another Social Movement.* ISA Convention, Panel "Global Capital, Global Labour"

Stiglitz, J. E. (1994) *Whither Socialism?* (London, The MIT Press)

Stillwell, F. (1999) *Globalisation: How Did We Get To Where We Are? (and Where Can We Go Now?).* http://phaa.net.au/conferences/stillwell.htm

Strange, S. (1988) *States and markets, an Introduction to International Political Economy.* (London, Pinter)

_____ **(1994)** *States and Markets (Second Edition).* (London, Pinter)

_____ **(1996)** *The Retreat of the State: The Diffusion of Power in the World Economy.* (Cambridge, Cambridge University Press)

_____ **(1997)** *Casino Capitalism.* (Manchester, Manchester university press)

_____(1998) *Mad Money.* (Manchester, Manchester university press)

Strange. S. and Stopford. J. (1991) *Rival states, Rival Firms: Competition for World Market Shares.* (Cambridge, Cambridge university press)

Stubbs, R. and Underhill, G. R. D. (eds.) (1994) *Political Economy and the Changing Global Order.* (Basingstoke, Macmillan)

_____ (2000), *Political Economy and the Changing Global Order 2nd edition.* (Basingstoke, Macmillan)

Taylor, R. (1994) *The Future of Trade Unions.* (London, Andre Deutsch)

Taylor, G. and Mathers, A. (2002) Social Partner or Social Movement? European Integration and Trade Union Renewal in Europe. *Labor Studies Journal, Vol. 27 No.1.*

Teague, P. and Grahl, J. (1992) *Industrial Relations and European Integration.*
(London, Lawrence and Fishart)

Terry, M. and Towers, B. (2000) Editorial: Developing Social Policy in the EU: Prospects and Obstacles. *Industrial Relations Journal, 31:4.*

Thair, T. and Risdon, A. (1999) Women in the Labour Market: Results from the Spring 1998 LFS. *Labour Market Trends, 107.*

Thomas, K. P. (1997) *Capital Beyond Borders: States and Firms in the Auto Industry, 1960-94.* (London, MacMillan)

Thompson, P. and Warhurst, W. (eds.) (1998) *Workplaces of the Future.*
(London, Macmillan)

Turner, L. (1996) *The Europeanisation of Labour: Structure Before Action.* In

Gabaglio, E and Hoffman, R. (eds.) (1998)

United Nations Conference on Trade and Development (1996) *World Investment Report 1996: Investment, Trade an International Policy Arrangements.* (New York and Geneva United Nations)

United Nations Development Programme (UNDP), (1995) *Human Development Report.* (New York, United Nations)

_____(1998) *Human Development Report.* (New York, United Nations)

Underhill, G. R. D. and Coleman, W. D. (eds.) (1998) *Regionalism and global economic integration: Europe, Asia and the Americas.* (London, Routledge)

Undy, R. (1999) Annual Review Article: New Labour's 'Industrial Relations Settlement': The Third Way? *British Journal of Industrial Relations, 37:2, June 1999.*

Vander Knaap, B. and Le Heron, R. (Eds.) (1995) *Human Resources and Industrial Spaces, a Perspective on Globalisation and Localisation.* (Chichester, John Wiley & Sons)

Van der Piijl, K. (1998) *Transnational Classes and International Relations.* (London, Routledge)

Van Parijs, P. (1993) *Marxism Recycled.* (Cambridge, Cambridge University Press)

Van Ruysseveldt, J. and Visser, J. (1996) *Industrial Relations in Europe: Traditions and Transitions.* (London, Sage)

Vogel, S. K. (1996) *Freer Markets, More Rules: Regulatory Reform in Advanced Industrial Countries.* (Athaca: Cornell)

Waddington, J. (1992) Trade Union Membership in Britain, 1980-1987: Unemployment and Restructuring. *British Journal of Industrial Relations, 30:2, June 1992.*

_____ (2000) Towards a Reform Agenda? European Trade Unions in Transition. *Industrial Relations Journal, 31:4.*

_____ (2001) Articulating Trade Union Organisation for the New Europe? *Industrial Relations Journal, 32:5.*

_____ (ed.) (1999) *Globalization and Patterns of Labour Resistance.*
(London, Mansell)

Waddington, J. and Hoffman, R. (eds.) (2000) *Trade Unions in Europe: Facing Challenges and Searching for Solutions.*
(Brussels, ETUI)

Waddington, J. and Whitson, C. (1997) Why Do People Join Unions in a Period of Membership Decline? *British Journal of Industrial Relations, 35:4, Dec 1997.*

Walker, R. J. B. (1993) *Inside/Outside: International Relations as Political Theory.* (Cambridge, Cambridge University Press)

_____ (1994) Social Movements/World Politics. *Millennium: Journal of International Studies. 23:3.*

Walters, S. (2002) Female Part-Time Workers' Attitudes to Trade Unions in Britain. *British Journal of Industrial Relations, 40:J, Mar 2002.*

Waterman, P. (1998) *Globalisation, Social Movements and the New Internationalisms.* (London, Mansell Publishing)

_____ (1999a) *Needed: A New International Labour Movement for (and against) a Globalised, Networked Capitalism.*
www.antenna.nl/-waterman/pages/peters/newinter.htm

_____ (1999b) *From Labour Internationalism to Global Solidarity.*
www .antenna.nll-waterman/pages.htm

_____ (2000) *Labour and Globalisation: The Dialogue of Which Millennium?* http:/llmedia.Nodong.net/archive/e 14.htm.

Waterman, and Wills, J. (eds.) (2001) *Place, Space and the New Labour Internationalisms.* (Oxford, Blackwell)

Waylen, G and Randall, V. (1998) *Gender, Politics and the State.* (New York, Routledge)

Weiss. L. (1998) *The Myth of the Powerless State: Governing the Economy in a Global Era.* (Cambridge, Cambridge polity press)

Whittock, M. (2000) *Feminising the Masculine? Women in Non-Traditional Employment.* (Aldershot, Ash gate)

Wichterich, C. (2000) *The Globalized Woman, Reports from a Future of Inequality.* (London, Zed Books)

Wilkinson, R. and Hughes, S. (2000) *Labour Standards and Global Governance: Examining the Dimensions of International Engagement.* Global Governance, 6, 2000: 259-277.

Williams, S. (1997) *The Nature of Some Recent Trade Union Modernization Policies in the UK.* British Journal of Industrial Relations, 35:4, Dec 1997.

Windmuller, J. P. Pursey, S. K. and Baker, J. (2014) *The International Trade Union Movement* in Blanpain, R. eds. (2014) Comparative Labour Law and Industrial Relations in Industrialized Market Economies, pp. 75–100

Wood, E. M. (1995) *Democracy Against Capitalism: Renewing Historical Materialism.* (Cambridge: Cambridge University Press

Wood, S. Moore, S. and Willman, P. (2002) *Third Time Lucky for Statutory Union Recognition in the UK?* Industrial Relations Journal, 33:3.

Zysman. J. (1983) *Governments, markets and growth: financial systems and the politics of industry.* (London: Robertson)

_____ (1996) *The Myth of a Global Economy: Enduring National Boundaries and Emerging Regional Realities.* New Political Economy, vol. 1, no.2.

_____ (1983) Governments, Markets and Growth; Financial Systems and the Politics of Industrial Change. (London, Cornell University Press)

PRESS RELEASES AND OTHER PRIMARY DOCUMENTATION

Department of Business, Energy and Industrial Strategy (DBEIS) (2017) *Trade Union Membership 2017 Statistical Bulletin.*
Https://assets.publishing.service.gov.uk/government/uploads/system/uploads/attachment_data/file/712543/TU_membership_bulletin.pdf

Department of Trade and Industry (DTI) (1998) *Fairness at Work. White Paper.* (London, HMSO)

_____(1999) *Working for the Future: the changing face of work practices,* DTI Publication URN 99/514. (London, HMSO)

EFILWC (1997) *European Super Unions on the Horizon?* (Dublin, EFILWC)

EIRO Online (1997a) *The Beginnings of Social Dialogue.*
www .eiro.eurofound.ie

_____ (1997b) *New Labour Aims to Sever its Roots?*
www .eiro.eurofound.ie

_____ (1998a) *Working Time Directive Implemented in the UK.*
www .eiro.eurofound.ie

_____(1998b) *Industrial Relations Under New Labour: an Update.*
www.eiro.eurofound.ie

(1999) *Trade Union Recognition and the Employment Relations Bill.* www.eiro.eurofound.ie

_____ (1999a) *Employment Relations Act Starts to Take Effect.*
www .eiro.eurofound.ie

_____(1999b) *Trade Unions Debate Future Strategy.*

www .eiro.eurofound.ie

_____ (1999c) *Union Membership Steadies after 18 years Decline.*
www .eiro.eurofound.ie

_____ (1999d) *Strikes in the UK: Withering away?*
www .eiro.eurofound.ie

(2000) *2000 Annual Review for the UK.* www.eiro.eurofound.ie

_____ (2000a) *Round up of Industrial Relations Developments.*
www .eiro.eurofound.ie

_____ (2001) *Employment Bill Published.*
www.eiro.eurofound.ie

_____ (2001a) *Unions Review Links With New Labour.*
www .eiro.eurofound.ie

_____ (2001b) *2001 Annual Review for the UK.*
www.eiro.eurofound.ie

_____ (2001c) *More Employers Recognising Union Reports TUC.*
www .eiro.eurofound.ie

ETUC (1997) *Our Priorities: ETUC Resolutions.* (Brussels, ETUC)

_____ (1998) *Trade Union Organisations and Decentralised Co-operation.*
(Brussels, ETUC)

_____ (1999a) *Aims and Objectives.* (Brussels, ETUC)

_____ (1999b) Press Release, *Gabaglio Calls for Closer Co-operation with European Parliament.*
http://etuc.org/press/highlight.

_____(1999c) Press Release, *EUIACP Co-operation Must Serve Social and Economic Development.* http://etuc.org/press/highlight.

_____(1999d) Press Release, *Labour Standards Must Apply in International Trade.* http://etuc.org/press/highlight.

_____ (1999e) *ETUC Statement to Cologne European Council.* http://etuc.org/press/highlight.

_____(19990 *The European Works Council by Order of the Law.* (Brussels, ETUC)

_____ (1999g) *Members of the ETUC.* (Brussels, ETUC).

_____(2000) *Trade Union Report: Conotou Agreement Joint with ICFTU and WCL.* (Brussels, ETUC)

ICFTU (2000) *Globalising Social Justice: Trade Unionism in the 21st Century* (Brussels, ICFTU)

_____(2000a) *The Union Movement is Changing Shape.* www.ICFTU.org

_____ (2000b) *Female Labour Activity.* www.ICFTU.org

_____(2001) *Slow Progress Towards Gender Equality.* www.icftu.org/jobs

ILO (1998) *World of Work, No. 23.* www.ilo.org/public/english/magazine

_____(1999) *World of Work No. 32.* www.ilo.org/public/english/magazine

_____(2000a) *The Impact of European Integration on the Development of National Labour Markets.* http://ILO.org.

_____(2000b) *ILO and the European Union Enlargement Process.* ILO: http://ILO.org.

_____(2000c) *What We Do.* ILO: http://ILO.org.

_____(2000d) *Major Programme 280. Field Programmes in Europe.* (Geneva, ILO)

_____(2000e) *ILO's Declarations, Conventions and Recommendations.* (Geneva, ILO)

SID (1997) *Labour Visions and Strategies for the 2F^1 Century: A Social Democratic Document.* http://www .laboumet.org/documents.

Somavia, J. (1999a) *Speech of Juan Somavia to the Congress of the European Trade Union Confederation (ETUC).* http://ILO.org/public/speeches.

_____(1999b) *Trade Unions in the 2Ft Century.* http://ILO .org/public/speeches.

TUAC (1997) *Trade Unions and Globalisation: Labour Markets and Structural Change.* http://www.tuac.org.

TUC (1989) *Europe 1992: Progress Report on Trade Union Objectives.* (London: TUC)

_____(1999) Press Release *"Partners not Poodles"* 28/6/1999. http://www. tuc.org.uk.

_____ (1999a) Press Release *"John Monks Keynote Speech to the ETUC".* http://www.tuc.org.uk.

UN (1999) Press Release, *Secretary General Proposes Global Compact on Human Rights, Labour, Environment, in Address to World Economic Forum.* http://www.un.org/news/press/docs.

_____(2000a) Press Release, *Secretary General, International Trae Union Representatives, Discuss Global Compact at*

Headquarters Meetzng. http://www.un.org/news/press/docs

_____ **(2000b)** Press Release, *Delivering Hendrik Brugman's Memorial Lecture, Deputy Secretary General Stresses that World Community Should be Firmly Based on Shared Values.* http://www.un.org/news/press/docs.

_____ **(2000c)** Press Release, *Deputy Secretary-General, Addressing Individual Human Rights and Forces of Globalisation, Stresses Need for long-term Thinking and Planning.* http://www.un.org/news/press/docs.

WCL (1997) *Report on Trade Union Rights Worldwide -1996-1997.*
http://www.cmt-wcl.org/en/pubs.

_____ **(1999a)** Press Release, *WCL asks IMF to Respect Social Fundamentals.*
(Brussels, WCL)

_____ **(1999b)** Press Release, *WCL Demands Social Standards in Trade Agreements, Under fLO Control.* (Brussels, WCL)

_____ **(2001)** *The Policy Resolution and the Topical Resolutions of the WCL: 25th congress of the WCL.* (Brussels, WCL)

_____ **(2001a)** *Women in the Informal Economy.* (Brussels, WCL)

_____ **(2003)** *Between Porto Alegre and Davos: Neo-Liberal globalisation no Longer Inspires Confidence.* (Brussels, WCL)

WIEGO (2001) *Globalization and the Informal Economy: how global trade and investment impact on the working poor.* www.wiego.org

_____ **(2003a)** *Fact Sheets, the informal economy.* www.wiego.org/main/fact

_____ **(2003b)** *Fact Sheets: women in the informal economy.* www.wiego.org/main/fact

_____ (2003c) *Fact Sheets: Home-Based Workers.* www.wiego.org/main/fact

_____(2003d) *Notes on trade unions and the informal sector* www.wiego.org/main/fact

_____(2003g) *Programme Areas.* www.wiego.org/main/areas

_____ (2003h) *SEWA (self employed women's association.* www.wiego.org/main/membersewa

WTO (1999) Press Release, *Labour Issue is False Debate.* (New York, WTO)